FROM BARSOOM TO MALACANDRA

MUSINGS ON THINGS PAST AND THINGS TO COME

JOHN C. WRIGHT

Wisecraft

CONTENTS

To Andrew and Bryanna Craig
without whose generosity this work might never have seen the light
of day.

A PRINCESS OF MARS

WELL, that day which every science fiction Dad looks forward-to has finally arrived at the Wright Household. For bedtime stories, I have previously read to my children such works as *Wonderful Flight to the Mushroom Planet* by Eleanor Cameron (where the Mushrooms are the good guys) and *The Gammage Cup* by Carol Kendall (where the Mushrooms are the bad guys) and, best of all, *The Mad Scientists' Club* by Bertrand R. Brinley (where the Mad Scientists are the good guys).

All this was merely to lay the groundwork. This day I started telling my youngest son, whom we have named Number Three Son Wright, all about *A Princess of Mars*. He became interested in the story, and so I pounced, and I read him the first five or so chapters last night. I don't own a copy myself, but the work is pre-1929, and in the public domain, so I printed it off the Gutenberg Project site, may God bless their efforts.

I read my boy his first honest-to-Barsoom sci fi book. This day, he is one of us, no more to be counted among the muggles. KAOR!

He was so taken by the story that he insisted I draw for him the Thark and the Calot and the other Martian life described in the book, and he insisted that he would invent a game like D&D but where you are transported to other worlds to spelunk in the buried cities and encounter hostile monstrosities, starting with Mars.

I was also taken by the story, and this came as a surprise.

Well, let me tell you, I had forgotten how good this book is. We fancy-pantsy elitist intellectuals (and I include myself) who read Homer in Greek and Milton in, uh, English, tend to look down our supercilious noses at mere pulp writing, but we hard-working sciffy lowbrow hack-writers (and I include myself) should pause to admire the economy and craftsmanship of this seminal work of scientifiction.

I thought I liked this book. No. Upon rereading it, I realize I love it. Let me tell you, dear reader, why.

The story opens with the cryptic line explaining that the narrator does not age, has no memory of being a child, and is a century old, or many centuries.

The action opens in the Old West of 1866, just after the Civil War, when the Confederation captain John Carter of Virginia, finding himself without a trade in peacetime, and the cause to which his sword had been pledged abolished, seeks his fortune in gold mining in the territories; the reader is lulled, or thrilled, into thinking this is merely one more Western Adventure tale, since the whole of the first chapter concerns John Carter's vain attempt to rescue his partner from being captured and tortured to death by Apaches, and he sets out in a cross-country trek by moonlight.

Let me just tell you, dear reader, that Indians never seem scary until you are reading about them to a young child, who, not being infected with the poison of Political Correctness, regards the prospect of being captured and tortured slowly to death as a serious drama, not as a cliché nor an insult to the savage warriors who (in real life, I should mention) practiced such dark deeds.

In chapter two, the story changes again, into some sort of Edgar Allen Poe or Arthur Machen tale of mystery and horror, as our hero, venturing into an empty but once-inhabited cave, is overcome by a mephitic fume of some sort, as lies paralyzed, awake and eyes opened, while the Apache gather at the cave mouth, terrified by whatever apparition they, but not the narrator, and not the reader, see with sadistic slowness and deliberation creeping toward our helpless protagonist.

Then our hero dies the death, and stands naked and looking down at his own corpse, fully clothed and motionless. Yet instead of being a spirit or shade, our hero is still breathing, possessed of a heartbeat, and every evidence of life.

Then he steps outside, sees the Red Planet low on the horizon, mystic, wonderful, alluring, dreadful, and raises his arms as if in salute or prayer to the pagan god of his profession, the soldier's god Mars. Then he wakes on that remote sphere, a landscape coated with yellowish-red moss, near the incubator of the four-armed goggle-eye Martians; he finds he cannot walk under the low gravity of Mars, as all his muscular habits are wrong, and must relearn the art like a baby; he is nearly speared by an adult band coming silently upon him, riding a fantastical many-legged cavalry; and he is taken prisoner into the vast ruins of an aeons-old civilization, domes of ivory and gold, that these gigantic greenish savages in nowise could have built.

To you, if you are a fan of science fiction, the scenario might seem trite. All I can report is that the reason why these books have remained in print for nigh a century is that the author does very well and very handily what he sets out to do.

3

If you think it is easy, you try it.

Let me mention, and I do not mean to pick on the fellow, that I have just this month read Michael Moorcock's pastiche and homage to Burroughs, *Warriors of Mars*, *Blades of Mars* (also published as *City of the Beast*, *Lord of the Spiders*) and found that it utterly failed to hold my interest. I don't think of myself as that hard to please—I like complex themes and daring insights into human nature and literary allusions as much as the next pencil-necked bespectacled intellectual, but I also read books like *The Shadow's Shadow* by Maxwell Grant for pleasure, not to mention comic books and other cotton candy of the land of letters.

But Moorcock could not carry it off. He tried and failed.

(No dishonor to Moorcock! The man is a masterful writer himself, the father of a literary movement, the inventor of some of the best beloved and well-remembered characters in the sci-fi pantheon. But in this case, he failed to achieve the desired effect.)

Let me mention a single example of one of the literary problems with this type of adventure story, a problem Burroughs solves handily, but which Moorcock does not.

In a first-person adventure tale, the hero must be heroic, but being in first person, he cannot seem to brag or boast, as nothing is more annoying (as we can tell by listening to the lyrics of half the rap songs on the radio these days).

Burroughs handles this by a bit of self-deprecating humor at that outset: when John Carter charges alone by moonlight, armed only with carbine, in the camp of some four hundred deadly savage Apache warriors, he calmly tells the reader that he is *not* brave, on account of the fact that he did not think about merely sneaking away and leaving his partner to his grisly fate until sometime the next day.

Carter as if reluctantly admits that honor is "something of a fetish" with him, but again he says (or jests) that it is a character flaw, because he cannot imagine behaving any other way.

Burroughs also handles the paradox of having a brave first-person narrator not call himself brave by describing Carter's reaction to being paralyzed in the cave: he admits his fear and terror at that time, but of course, this is an almost supernatural terror, very different from the type of threats an active man armed with courage in his heart and steel in his hand can face.

There is a next scene where one of the gigantic Green Men of Mars yanks Carter roughly by the arm, commanding him to perform his antics of jumping for the Thark Chieftain: Carter not only answers the brute by breaking his jaw with a fist, but he fully expects to die for his act, putting his back to the wall and resolving to kill as many of the foe as he might before he falls under their greater numbers.

Now, the kind of character who is willing to die rather than to be manhandled or enslaved is quite slippery, by which I mean it is far too easy to slip up, and leave the reader thinking the attitude is corny, one-dimensional, or unbelievable. But this scene takes place one chapter after we saw the same hero in the cave of fear, petrified literally and figuratively. The craftsmanship of the contrast makes the courage of the second scene seem more realistic.

Again, John Carter also risks death to save the corpse of his fallen friend, not wishing the body to be savaged or mutilated by the Red Indians (who have no more notion of civilized or Christian practices than, say, your average modern man raised with modern pseudo-scientific education). It is a gesture that shows Carter to be a man who values something nobler and greater than his own gross bodily pleasures, vainglorious self-esteemery, and trivial worldly self-interests without the first-person narrator needing to explain or emphasize the point.

Modern readers who have no idea what honor is need not be distracted by the point, because it passes by so quickly, and can merely enjoy the action, whose pace, by the way, never slows.

Moorcock, on the other hand, does nothing to establish his character Kane as being a man of honor or a man of particular courage before he is transported to Mars. Michael Kane is a professor working on a teleportation machine, whose malfunction sends him back to Mars of the ancient past, when it was still a green and inhabited world.

Moorcock does have Kane say, at one point, that he yearns to return to Old Mars, not only because his lady love is there, but because the sense of honor he finds nowhere on Earth, there still holds true. This is a very stirring sentiment, and it captures in one line the heart and soul of what makes Planetary Romances and all Burroughseque yarns appealing: they are meant to be the romance and danger of the Old West in SPA-AA-ACE, when men were men, and honor was honor.

The problem with Kane's statement is that the book in which he appears does not bear this out: neither the Argzoon nor the other foes of the City of the Green Mists have any particular sense of honor or chivalry, nor does Kane himself risk anything or make any gestures in that direction, except, perhaps, once, when he interrupts a domestic dispute between Shizala (the space princess of this epic) and her fiancée: but the point of the scene is undercut, first, because Kane is portrayed as a dope who does not realize the obvious: neither that he loves Shizala, nor she him, nor that she is engaged: and second, because he is upbraided by the space dame for his clumsy interruption.

The contrast is between a man who smites a brutal captor and expects to die for it and a man who interrupts a domestic quarrel and beats a cad manhandling his (the cad's) betrothed. The second example rings a bit hollow, doesn't it? It is the kind of thing someone from the Hippie Generation thought someone from the Victorian Generation acted like, but not what they actually acted like, which is more represented by the first example.

Likewise, when John Carter first addresses Dejah Thoris, he speaks in words rare or impossible to see these days: "Suffice it, for the present, that I am your friend, and, so far as our captors will permit, your protector and your servant."

Michael Kane of Old Mars I am sure is a fine and stalwart fellow, but he does not express his love for his princess by declaring himself her friend, protector, and servant. That ideal comes from a more civilized era.

The point of fact is that Burroughs actually "gets" the concept of the honorable soldier, and naturally has his characters act this way; whereas Moorcock, writing half a century later, regards the concept, perhaps, in this case, fondly, but from the point of view of an outsider, and his characters only pay it lip-service. He is not sympathetic to the concept of heroism, even if he wants to be: he does not "get it".

Moorcock is of course at a terrific disadvantage. When one sits down to write a pastiche, one deliberately set's one's imagination to be unimaginative. The tale must follow a model of the original. But the original is actually original.

How original? When I read the scene to my boy where Carter learns that all Green Men are raised from eggs indifferently by all the women of the tribe, no man knowing mother or father, but all children merely raised in common by the community, and defective eggs smashed or children abandoned and left to die of exposure by the eugenics of the Green Men, he was properly horrified. When Dejah Thoris pleads with the Green Men for peace and amity between their peoples, she specifically identifies the communal lifestyle, the communism or Spartanism, as the trait that has driven all finer emotion, family love, fellowship, and friendship out of the Green race. Rereading this with adult eyes, I was struck to the core by the clarity of the insight. These words were written in 1912.

One pivotal character whom I did not recall from when I read this in my youth was Sola, the Green Martian woman who tends and teaches John Carter during his captivity. She is explicitly said to be an atavism or throwback from a million years ago, when Mars had water, and softer emotions still existed. (It is later revealed that she, unlike her peers, actually recalls her father and mother.)

My young son was properly outraged when one of the reptile-hearted women of the tribe dismissed Sola's sympathy and mercy as degenerate, and their own Spartan or Soviet inhumanity and cruelty as progress. Number Three Son exclaimed in indignation, "Don't they realize they are just going *backwards*!" (I explained that all corruption is described as progress by the Progressives.) He was disheartened to hear that the Green Men did not reform by the end of the series.

This tale fathered its own genre called Planetary Romance, or Sword-and-Planet adventures, in much the same way that Tolkien fathered the genre of High Fantasy: but their flatterers and imitators in both cases imitated surface features and missed the pith. Tolkien's masterwork is about the fortitude to endure when all hope is lost. Burrough's is about honor. If the writer of an homage or pastiche does not take fortitude or honor seriously, his homage will be no real homage.

Let me emphasize that those tropes which seem to us trite were first invented, and used and re-used, because they solved certain difficulties which otherwise hindered the reader's enjoyment of the tale being hammered together.

The Green-skinned men of Mars, for example, are perhaps the first depiction of an otherwordly species which is both exotic enough to excite wonder, human enough to be human, and not supernatural. Their hairlessness, bulging eyes that operate independently of each other, savage tusks, great height and extra pair of limbs, described (at least at first) as being either arms or legs, creates quite a different impression than, for example, H.G. Wells' depiction of a creature composed almost entirely of brain, with hands of great strength and sensitivity.

Wells' Martians are simply monsters. They are the image, or the nightmare, of what Darwinian theory would portray future man or superman to be: as the Englishman was thought to be less robust than the caveman, the future man would likewise be more delicate and less hirsute than the Englishman. As the brain and the hands of man granted Man's dominion over the Earth, likewise the older planet Mars, suffering a longer span of evolutionary ascension, would bring forth a master race of greater brains and finer fingers.

(Let me correct one word: "Darwinism" properly so called is a biological theory which makes no predictions. You need crackpot philosophers, Hegel or Nietzsche or Marx, or playwrights like Shaw, to propose a theory that evolution is directed to the end of producing finer or more manlike descendants to Man. Wells was playing off this popular yet false conception of directed Darwinian evolution. He plays with the theory more honestly by predicting the Morlocks and Eloi of *The Time Machine*.)

But I am lost in a digression: the point here is that Wellsian Martians never speak, and if they did, it would break the spell. They would seem less horrifying, less supremely ultra-evolved than man. They would just be bald men with big heads, as, indeed, the countless copies of Wells made them out to be in later books and comics.

But by adding limbs and tusks and removing hair, Burroughs creates something alien and savage, but at the same time human enough to make Tars Tarkas not merely a character, but a man of honor and a warrior worthy of fellowship and admiration: yet a character no less appalling and impressive than some giant or titan, a Goliath or a Svargotyr, from tales of old.

Why green? Nowadays the concept of green men from Mars is so trite as to be a joke. But the hue is innately alien and jarring, not being white, black, red, or yellow. Why extra limbs? It is a quick and elegant solution to make the Martian beasties seem unearthly without making them so unlike anything we know that the reader has no stock emotional reaction to them: an eight-legged hairless horse critter, or a ten-legged lizardy lion will still carry the connotations of horse and lion to the reader without further ado.

Again, with the depiction of Mars as an ancient, dying planet, peopled by forgotten races clinging by means of failing technology to a depleting atmosphere, Burroughs creates a setting so memorable, so eerie, so melancholy, and yet with such promise of romance, action, and adventure, that he solves at one stroke the several problems of how to please those readers who wish for swordfights as of the days of yore, those who wish for radium-pistols or flying machines as of things to come, the antiquity of Angkor Wat and forgotten cities of the jeweled and perfumed jungles of the Far East, the romance of the savage wilderness of the Old West, and so on. Future and past, East and West, everything is neatly drawn up in a single and elegant concept: Mars is ancient and senile, a dying world, noble as Rome eroding into a Dark Ages, with Viking and Paynim on opposite horizons: a time fit for a warlord who worships the war god.

FROM BARSOOM TO MALACANDRA

Has the concept, or others of his, been overused and shop-worn? If you read to your child, you will find they are as fresh and new as springtime, which indeed returns every year, but indeed is ever new.

What is the appeal of such books? Oh, come now.

Bloodshed, Monsters, Honor, Savagery, True Love, Dying Cities, Flying Machines and Naked Folk Armed to the Teeth. What is not to like?

One final thought:

Number Three Son and I were reading to Chapter XI of Princess of Mars, when we came across these words. John Carter is trying to explain his origins to Dejah Thoris.

She addresses him thus:

"I heard your challenge to the creature you call Tars Tarkas, and I think I understand your position among these people, but what I cannot fathom is your statement that you are not of Barsoom."

"In the name of my first ancestor, then," she continued, "where may you be from? You are like unto my people, and yet so unlike. You speak my language, and yet I heard you tell Tars Tarkas that you had but learned it recently. All Barsoomians speak the same tongue from the ice-clad south to the ice-clad north, though their written languages differ. Only in the valley Dor, where the river Iss empties into the lost sea of Korus, is there supposed to be a different language spoken, and, except in the legends of our ancestors, there is no record of a Barsoomian returning up the river Iss, from the shores of Korus in the valley of Dor. Do not tell me that you have thus returned! They would kill you horribly anywhere upon the surface of Barsoom if that were true; tell me it is not!"

Her eyes were filled with a strange, weird light; her voice was pleading, and her little hands, reached up upon my breast, were pressed against me as though to wring a denial from my very heart.

"I do not know your customs, Dejah Thoris, but in my own Virginia a gentleman does not lie to save himself; I am not of Dor;

I have never seen the mysterious Iss; the lost sea of Korus is still lost, so far as I am concerned. Do you believe me?"

My son and I, both gentlemen of Virginia, immediately rose to our feet, sang the anthem of the commonwealth, and made the salute, and shouted *Sic Semper Tyrannis.*

I laughed a laugh more cold and bitter, and I could not explain to my young son why I laughed when I read this line:

All property among the green Martians is owned in common by the community, except the personal weapons, ornaments and sleeping silks and furs of the individuals. These alone can one claim undisputed right to, nor may he accumulate more of these than are required for his actual needs. The surplus he holds merely as custodian, and it is passed on to the younger members of the community as necessity demands.

The women and children of a man's retinue may be likened to a military unit for which he is responsible in various ways, as in matters of instruction, discipline, sustenance, and the exigencies of their continual roamings and their unending strife with other communities and with the red Martians. His women are in no sense wives. The green Martians use no word corresponding in meaning with this earthly word. Their mating is a matter of community interest solely, and is directed without reference to natural selection. The council of chieftains of each community control the matter as surely as the owner of a Kentucky racing stud directs the scientific breeding of his stock for the improvement of the whole.

In theory it may sound well, as is often the case with theories, but the results of ages of this unnatural practice, coupled with the community interest in the offspring being held paramount to that of the mother, is shown in the cold, cruel creatures, and their gloomy, loveless, mirthless existence.

You see, I had read those theories, of Plato and of Marx, of the collectivist and eugenicist daydreams which form the major axis of the current secularist Progressivism which forms the most advanced of the several morbid cancers and diseases of which our current civilization is dying.

Burroughs saw clearly enough in 1912 what the terrible cost to the soul is exacted when the vain attempt is made to put into practice these Lacedaemonian infatuations.

2

YESTERDAY'S LONG-LOST
TOMORROW

TODAY, at the time of this writing, 6 January, is the Feast of the Epiphany, which celebrates the adoration of the Magi, the sorcerer-kings of the East, who had read in the conjunctions of the stars that a new king was born of Jewry, and trekked from the astronomical towers and cryptic libraries of Babylon to find him, beyond expectation, in the hovel of a cabinet maker.

Tradition names this as the last day of the Twelve Days of Christmas, the Twelfth Night, which of old was celebrated with a masquerade, servants dressed as masters, women as men and suchlike. The famed Shakespeare play, where Roselind goes garbed as Ganymede commemorates this cross-dressing antic.

It is therefore a fitting day to discuss the restoration of the 1927 silent film *Metropolis*. It is fitting because the film includes visions as prophetic as anything an astrologer could dream, including a tower fittingly called "Neubabelsberg" or "The New Tower of Babel" and including the Twelfth Night masquerade deception of a machine man dressed as a maiden.

For those of you unfamiliar with the story, *Metropolis* is the masterpiece of the German Expressionist film maker, some would say genius, Fritz Lang, who also made "M" and the *Doctor Mabuse* films.

If you do not know who Fritz Lang is, if you have ever seen, perhaps on an old *Flintstones* cartoon or a skit from a comedy show, the image of a Hollywood director in jodh-purs with a German accent and a monocle—that German is Fritz Lang. That stereotyped caricature of a Hollywood director in a monocle is Fritz.

Fritz Lang himself fled Germany the same night he was offered a post by the Nazis in their new regime. During the Weimar years, between the wars, Germany was the center of the brief but brilliant and seminal silent film Golden Age, producing such masterworks as *The Cabinet of Dr. Caligari* and *Das Nibelungen* and *Nosferatu*. Silent films were easier to export than later talkies, because only the title cards needed to be changed. Unfortunately, it also made them easier to edit.

Metropolis was the most expensive film ever shot in its day (some five million Reichsmarks) and it opened in a lavish theater, with a live orchestra playing an original score. It was originally 153 minutes long, but was cut—I would say butchered—into a shorter 90 minute version, and the plot changed—I would say mutated into grotesque illogic, if not lobotomized. The American version was rewritten by the playwright Channing Pollick, whose name should live in infamy, or, at least, serve as a warning to science fiction visionaries not to allow mundane minds a chance to meddle with our work.

About a fourth of the original film was lost, apparently forever. Brave efforts were made to deduce what the original plot had been when antiquarians would find, for example, the wording of the original title cards in old records in the

German censor's office, or notations on the orchestral score, where brief descriptions of the action on the screen were written in the margins to tell the orchestra leader when to play certain themes, high notes, or flourishes to match the screen action.

Then, in 2008, one canister in a forgotten museum collection in Buenos Aires was noticed to be too large. The label listing the running time showed that this version of *Metropolis* was some thirty minutes longer than any surviving copy. In great excitement it was discovered that the missing scenes were back.

Why such excitement? This was the first and biggest and most lasting depiction of the future on film. I will be bold enough to say that the visual images we still carry in our heads of what the future in the year 2000 will be (images that are now oddly retro-futuristic) of elevated roadways and soaring super-skyscrapers and flocks of biplanes darting between the towers, visualizations of video-telephones, mechanical men and mad scientists and massive machinery looming in Morlockian underworlds, all derive from the art direction of *Metropolis*.

I suggest that the magazine cover images from the days of pulp adventures and popular science come from this film, not the other way around. Hugo Gernsbeck's magazine *Amazing* was founded in 1926, only twelve months before the release of Lang's film.

Look at the visual imagery of everything from *The Jetsons* to the Trantor-ripoff imperial world-city Coruscant in *Star Wars*. To this day, when one thinks of the lands of the future, one imagines super skyscrapers, elevated highways, and flying machines.

The modern filmgoer who lives in the days of computer graphics, deeply impressed with the visual splendor of James Cameron's *Avatar* is no doubt wondering why anyone would be interested in the clunky and unconvincing visual effects of a silent movie. As to that, all I can say is that the visual effects here were done with care and craftsmanship and imagination, and my eye, at least, is fooled by the models and cunning tricks with mirrors. For example, to make the traffic move on the imaginary elevated roadway, the city scene was painted on glass, the road was left clear, and a mirror behind was set to reflect a tabletop model on which the prop vehicles moved.

Also, the opening shot shows an expressionist painting of a cityscape where the shadows slide across the walls and windows of the image. This is, in fact, the first known example of stop motion animation, a process invented for this shot. I can speak for no other viewer than myself, but whenever I see the first time some technique has been done, it still seems fresh and wonderful to me, even if I had seen it done countless times before.

But one must be warned that silent films are an acquired taste. The "acting" consists of broad pantomime motions meant to be seen by theater's back row. To indicate that a man was falling in love, for example, the actor clutches his heart with both hands and goggles his eyes like a sick cow, holding the pose frozen for many lingering moments.

Because one cannot hear the actress scream, she must gape her mouth and roll her eyes, arms overhead, fingers spread, and fling herself from one side of the frame to the other, hyperventilating in hyper-terror for many lingering moments.

This is after she walks through the catacombs for lingering minutes with a candle, being chased by a circle of light from a flashlight. The key word here is lingering. Fritz Lang was not the master of the MTV style "quick cut." The film is slow, moody, and atmospheric, and could be called a Gothic as easily as a Science Fiction piece.

The convention of female film beauty in the 1920's is as odd to the modern eye as the conventional makeup of a geisha girl: flat-chested, thin-hipped with pale and narrow-lipped faces like something from an Aubrey Beardsley ink drawing and wearing your great grandmother's hairstyle.

Appreciating the plot of a silent film is also an acquired taste. The story has to be told almost entirely in images, with only brief one-sentence snatches of dialog. Consequently, plots tend toward broad operatic melodrama.

The screenplay was written by Prussian actress Thea von Harbou, Lang's wife, who apparently favored the Ayn Rand approach to putting across her point. Here, the moral of the story is showed to the audience in the opening, repeated throughout, and forms the final curtain line. *Between the head and the hands, the heart must mediate.* If the moral had been written on a two by four and smashed into my head between the eyes over and over again, it could not have been made more obvious. Subtlety is not the strong point of this screenplay.

Nonetheless, my appreciation of the restored versionis precisely because the butchered version of the plot made no sense. More on this later.

Thea von Harbou later joined the National Socialist or Nazi Party, and her view of the relation between workers and owners is correspondingly socialist: the proles are mere worker ants despised and crushed by the plutocrats who live in sybaritic decadence.

The main plot tension is between the ultra-rich owning and ruling class of the futuristic mega-city, personified in Joh Frederson (called John Masterman in the English version) and the downtrodden proletarian workers, who trudge in endless drudgery in their buried caverns and subterranean factories, personified in the beautiful Maria.

The handsome son of Joh Frederson, Freder, falls in love

at first sight with Maria, and his conscience is provoked by her tale of the brotherhood of man, and by pity for the wretched overworked and dangerous lives of the dispossessed, compared to the endless gaiety and frivolity of the life of the sons of wealth and privilege, such as his own.

The proletarians are meeting in secret, murmuring against their oppression, inching toward violence (despite the voice of Maria, who preaches mediation and reconciliation), and Frederson is taking steps to quell the discontented, but not quelling the discontent. These steps include turning to Rotwang the Inventor, a maimed and brilliant genius, who has invented a machine-man that can perfectly impersonate a human being. So Freder is torn between his duty to his father and his feelings for his beloved.

This admittedly simplistic tale of socialism and social conscience is told in luxurious Biblical imagery that I simply did not expect to see: The metropolis of Neubabelsberg is the Tower of Babel, a work of ambition displaying the greatness of Man, but destined to destruction at the hands of the workers, agents of divine vengeance, in an Apocalypse brought on by the Whore of Babylon, who in this case is the femm-bot invented by Rotwang the Inventor.

The only hope to avert destruction is the voice of divine conscience, personified by the virgin Maria, who preaches in the underground catacombs as if still hiding from the persecution of Nero, with the crosses of Calvary rising in the background.

The statues representing the Seven Deadly Sins and the Grim Reaper spring to life in one hallucination sequence, and the final fight between the hero and the mad inventor takes place on the sloping roof of a Cathedral, beneath the scowling stone eyes of Apostles and Archangels.

It is strange for a man living in a post-Christian and Christophobic era to see a film made in a Christian era, when the audience was assumed to be familiar with the Bible and Biblical imagery, and to react not with scorn and derision, but with affection, to those images. A modern and openly Christian film would not introduce such images so unselfconsciously, without any explanation, because the modern audience must be assumed to be ignorant and hostile. The vocabulary of images is closed to them.

The inventor, Rotwang, is simply the icon of the Mad Scientist. He is the first and the best. He is played by Rudolf Klein-Rogge, an actor of brutally handsome features who also played the arch-villain in *Doctor Mabuse the Gambler* (A film that got Fritz Lang in trouble with the rising Nazi Party bosses, for its portrayal of unscrupulous powerlust against a backdrop of decadence).

I will wager that the average reader, reading the words "Mad Scientist" unknowingly conjures up a mental image that was invented by Rotwang the Inventor. Here we can see what the stylized overacting and the stylized expressionism of silent film are trying to accomplish: you, the audience, are able to tell at first glance which is the Mad Inventor and which is the stoical Arch-Industrialist.

The deep and staring eyes that range from brooding to maniacal, the egotism, the wild hair, the soulless genius: all come from here. Like Davros the creator of the Daleks from *Doctor Who*, Rotwang is a cripple, the imperfection of his flesh an unsubtle symbol of inner imperfection. Like Doctor No from the Bond film of the same name, Rotwang sports a creepy mechanical hand. (Futuristically enough for a 1920's film, this is a prosthetic or cyberorganic hand, not a mere hook.)

There is even a scene where he cackles, exalting, that the loss was well worth the triumph of learning to create artificial, mechanized life. An imitator of God who creates a golem or mockery of life is a shade of Doctor Victor von Frankenstein.

As befits the Gothic look of the film, the lair of Rotwang the Inventor is a crooked medieval alchemists' workshop, crammed with books (or should I say "grimoires"?) and decorated with satanic pentacles. In the middle of an Art Deco city of skyscrapers and aeroplanes, crouches a single house from the Dark Ages.

The first time I saw this film (if memory serves, on a PBS station when I was a teen) it was of course the butchered version, not knowing there once was (or once was supposed to be) any other. Since I was used to sudden leaps of illogic in the badly-done monster films that passed for sci-fi back in the old days, I did not see anything amiss.

Having seen the restored version let me report that I am now personally offended at Mr. Channing Pollick, and would be willing to lead an Orwellian "Two Minute Hate" excoriating his name, because I now see what was cut and changed.

Both versions open the same way. We see the proles marching, heads bowed, likes slaves to the silver mines, in shambling lines to the elevators descending into the underworld, where they tend giant machines designed to explode whenever momentary inattention allows a clearly-labeled thermometer or pressure gauge to reach the clearly-labeled "explode immediately" position.

In shining towers high above, young noblemen indulge in athletics and flirt with gardens of courtesans. Our heroine, Maria, leads a dirt-smudged gaggle of Oliver Twist lookalikes up through an elevator to gaze at the gardens, and our hero falls in love at first sight, as symbolized by clutching his heart in both hands and gazing like a moonstruck cow. She is tossed out by footmen, and he goes into the depths to look for her.

Like Buddha seeing life outside the pleasure palaces of his father for the first time, Freder encounters the misery and death on which his city, the Tower of Babel, is built: he sees an industrial accident, transformed before his hallucinating eyes into a vision of the great idol Moloch eating chained victims by the score.

Freder exchanges clothing with a worker, and spends a ten-hour work shift pushing arms on the pointless rotating thing machine. I am sure something will blow up if he fails to move the arms fast enough. Then he hallucinates that it is the ten-hour clock counting down the minutes to the shift change. Freder hallucinates a lot. You would think Joh Frederson his father would be more concerned.

Uber-plutocrat Joh Frederson goes to Rotwang the Inventor carrying a fragment of map found on the body of a dead proletarian (killed in the aforementioned industrial accident) and wishing to know its meaning.

At this point, the two versions part ways.

In the Channing Version, for no particular reason, Rotwang displays to Frederson his latest invention, the machine-man, which is supposed to be able to replace the workers at their dangerous tasks. Boasting about how his machine-man is the ultimate labor-saving if not life-saving device, Rotwang appears to be screaming in anger for no reason, his eyes aflame with arrogance, while Frederson hears him with stoical and understated grief.

Since this would, in fact, relieve the workers from the need to risk their lives tending the Moloch Machine, logically this would solve the problem driving the plot, and everyone would live happily ever after. But no.

Consulting the fragment of map, Rotwang and Frederson descend into the catacombs, and spy out a meeting of the proletarians. Maria tells of the legend of the Tower of Babel, and tells the proles to wait in joyous hope for a coming mediator or messiah, who will lead them peacefully to reconciliation with their brutal capitalist overlords.

Rotwang, but not Frederson, spots Freder among the listening crowd, and slyly steps to block the father's sight so that he does not see the son. This action has no meaning.

Frederson suddenly, and for no apparent reason, orders Rotwang to make the Machine Man into a perfect replica of Maria the leader of the proletarians. There is no hint beforehand that Rotwang, or anyone, has this technology. Maria, it must be emphasized, is asking the proles not to resort to violence, but Frederson now orders Rotwang to have the false Maria provoke the as-yet-peaceful proles into a violent rebellion. Against him. To overthrow him. Uh, what?

To prove to Frederson that the false Maria is convincing as a duplicate, Rotting displays her to the lustful audience at Yoshiwara in the decadent red-light district, and Frederson looks on in approval as the sons of his fellow industrialists are provoked into murderous jealousy against each other. Duels and murders follow. Uh, what?

Hugger-mugger and hurly-burly ensues. There are alarums and excursions. Freder falls ill for some reason I don't recall, and he spends some time in his room, pursuing his favorite pastime, hallucinating.

The prole rebellion happens as planned, the proles wreck the Heart Machine in order to stop the pumps that prevent their underground worker's town from being flooded. The flood that they brought upon themselves threatens their wives and moppets back in the dormitory.

Our Hero Freder, with the help from the real Maria, rescues the children of the workers from the rising waters. The Evil Robot version of Maria, whom I will call Nega-Maria, is captured and burnt at the stake as a witch, while Rotwang chases the real Maria across the roof of the cathedral.

There does not seem to be any particular reason why Rotwang, who was hired by Frederson to provoke the worker rebellion, to be pursuing Maria. But Freder arrives in time to save the day, and wrestles Rotwang. Since this was from the days before film makers knew how to capture a convincing fight scene on film, the scrimmage is awkward and unconvincing, but eventually Rotwang is flung to his death from the rooftop, and the girl is saved.

Joh Frederson and Grot the foreman are brought together by Freder the promised mediator, who makes them shake hands and vow to work together in love and brotherhood. *Between the head and the hands, the heart must mediate.* The End.

Uh, what?

As a child, pure and pure-hearted as all children, whenever I saw the movie *It's a Wonderful Life*, I always wondered why the evil banker, Potter, is allowed to keep the money he stole from the simpleminded Uncle Billy, rather than, as would have made more sense to my wee boyish brain and been more gratifying to my wee boyish heart, the avenging angel Clarence were to suddenly announce, "Potter stole the dough!" and all of Jimmy Stewart's friends, whose number makes him the richest man in town, would form a brutal vigilante mob, descend upon Potter, drag him from the wheelchair, and drown him in the swimming pool beneath the moving gymnasium floor. (I admit I was more gratified than the average viewer when SATURDAY NIGHT LIVE, did a "How It Should Have Ended" type skit where something very close to these bloody events unfolded.)

When I first saw *Metropolis* as a youth, being as pure and pure-hearted as all boys, I had exactly the same reaction. Even after the film ended, I kept expecting there to be a final scene where someone, perhaps Grot the Foreman, instead of shaking hands and vowing to work in brotherhood with Joh

Frederson would instead twist his arm behind his back and catch him by the throat.

After all, Joh Frederson is an arch-criminal madman who just hired a mad scientist madder than he to provoke the worker revolt that just deliberately led to the flood that almost drowned all the children, or, as we science fiction people call them, "Younglings."

Indeed, I, for one, would have rejoiced to see Joh Frederson confronted by his son, or the police, or the princess Padma Amidala, crying in anguished disbelief, "You killed the Younglings?!" and see the villain without more delay dragged (rolling his eyes and shrieking in the lovable over-acting way endemic to silent films) to the still smoking stake to burn him in the shadow of the Cathedral as a would-be mass murderer, while little dancing children threw matches and their smiling mothers threw winebottles filled with gasoline. But maybe that is just me.

But this did not happen. Instead they shake hands, and evil powermad Joh Frederson, would-be mass-child-murderer, failing to have destroyed himself and his own city, lives happily ever after.

Such is the Channing Version that the English-speaking world saw.

The father of science fiction, H.G. Wells, was among the reviewers who dismissed this plot as silly, and I, for one, agree with him. It is of course, the Channing plot he was dismissing, not the real plot.

In the Thea von Harbou Version, we see Uber-Plutocrat Joh Frederson go to Rotwang the Inventor, and, by mischance, Frederson comes upon a curtained alcove behind which he peers. In the alcove is an Art Deco larger-than-life death mask of his long-lost wife, Hel, staring down, immense, titanic, with blind eyes, set up as some sort of freakish love-idol.

Rotwang the Inventor discovers his widower-guest discovering his immense freakish love-idol to Frederson's own wife. Rotwang was also in love with her, but she died giving birth to Freder, the hated son of his hated rival. Wrathfully, Rotwang now boasts that he can replace Hel with his machine-man, an artificial life form designed to be able perfectly to impersonate a woman.

Next we see the machine-man, seated lifelessly beneath an occult pentacle, stir to an artificial mockery of life upon command, and stand, and walk. It turns its mask and regards Frederson with eyes as blind and eerie as the eyes of the titanic statue we just saw.

The scene is creepy as all get out.

Bad enough to visit your ex-best friend's house and find a giant idol of your dead wife, but then to find your ex-best friend is building a life-sized doll version of her, and is tampering, using dark forces, with the secrets of life and death. Oh, and he hates you. And he burnt off his hand in some unnamed science accident, but laughs and claims it was worth the price. For science!

In this version both the anger of Rotwang and the stoical sorrow of Frederson make sense, since they are discussing a dead woman beloved of both, rather than merely discussing the wisdom of deploying a labor-saving device.

Also in the von Harbou Version, Frederson makes the much more reasonable request to Rotwang to use his robot to impersonate Maria for the purpose of *quelling* the proletarian discontent, and breaking up the dangerous meetings, not aggravating it.

In the scene in the catacombs, Rotwang steps to block Frederson's view of Freder among the workers listening to Maria because Rotwang means to betray Frederson, using the robot not to quell the discontent but rather to stir it up. Rotwang's plan is to lure young Freder (who is in love with

Maria) to his doom, because, as has been clearly established in this version, Rotwang blames Freder for the death of Hel.

There is also a second plotline, again, one that in this version makes sense. Once Freder is overcome with sympathy for the proletarians, his suspicious father orders a creepy character called only "The Thin Man" (played by an actor with the glorious name Fritz Rasp) to follow young Freder and report on his movements.

Rasp (if I may use that name) discovers the substitution mentioned above, when Freder changes clothing and lives with a worker named 11811. Ironically, this worker uses the opportunity, and huge wad of cash found in Freder's suit, to visit the red light district called Yoshiwara, and fritter the night away in the soul-destroying pleasures of the upper town.

This location becomes significant later, as Rotwang's femm-bot Nega-Maria uses her Weimar-era flapper charms to seduce the young sons of privilege into dueling and fighting each other. This scene, which was senseless in the Channing Version, here makes sense because Rotwang's motive is to use the robot to destroy Frederson and his magnificent city from above as well as from below.

Her Art Deco L33t mad dancing Skillz make all eyes rivet upon her, as demonstrated in one of the freakier of the German Expressionist shots in the film: a shot composed entirely of unwinking, staring eyeballs.

Rasp also discovers that Freder has saved from suicide and hired Josaphat, the private secretary of Foreperson fired arbitrarily, and Josaphat is now Freder's manservant. Rasp is a ruthless operative, and forces Freder's new found friends away from him. This point is significant, since Freder falls into a lingering fever in the middle act, and Josaphat is forced to betray rather than help him.

Also in the Harbou Version, the rebellion of the workers

is established as a plot by Rotwang to the destroy the city, so that when Nega-Maria leads them to destroy the Heart Machine and flood the undertown, her purpose is to kill the workers, because (again) Rotwang is the arch enemy of Frederson and of the Metropolis.

The workers, convinced that they have been tricked by her into drowning their own children, chase the real Maria (whom they blame) up through the streets to Yoshiwara, where Nega-Maria is dancing for the sons of privilege. The real Maria escapes, and the mob ties Nega-Maria to the stake, where, before their horrified eyes, her burning flesh peels back to reveal the inhuman mask of the machine-man beneath.

The real Maria is trapped in the Cathedral by Rotwang, who has gone magnificently mad (a perennial hazard for those in the Mad Scientific community) and now is convinced that Maria is the real Hel.

The ending of both versions is the same: Freder wrestles Rotwang. Rotwang plunges like Lucifer in downfall from the cathedral roof. Frederson and Grot the Foreman are brought together by Freder the promised mediator, handshake, love and brotherhood. *Between the head and the hands, the heart must mediate.* The End.

This ending is somewhat more satisfying, because this time Frederson is the victim, rather than the boss, of Rotwang, and his only crime is his unwillingness to treat the proletarians with the simple dignity they deserve, and he is snapped out of that moral blindness by his loving son when he sees the tragic horror, manipulated by Rotwang, to which that cold-heartedness can lead.

The Channing Version cut out the character of Hel, the motive of Rotwang, and the whole plotline of twisted revenge by Rotwang against Frederson. Channing, in a surviving interview, commented that the idea of a man building a robot to be his substitute wife was absurd, even gross. Who would take a cold metallic body to the bridal bed?

Apparently Channing was too stupid to notice that in the climactic scene, the one best for which this film is best remembered, where the robot becomes the doppelganger of Maria, Rotwang has the ability to clothe the robotic skeleton with the flesh and blood form of any woman he desires.

The gross absurdity of the idea of marrying a moving machine-creature of one's own devising is a feature, not a bug, of the science fiction plot—we are supposed to find Rotwang's egotistical monomania for a dead woman creepy, and maybe a little sad.

But we are not supposed to think the goal is beyond his powers as a master of dark science. Rotwang was not planning on hugging and kissing the metal skeleton, as Channing thought. The Inventor was going to make her look like Hel, Frederson's beloved, but instead decided to make her look like Maria, Freder's beloved.

Since both versions show Rotwang perfectly able to make the femme-bot into a perfect impersonation of a woman, Channing's grounds for cutting that part out, the idea that the idea was absurd, is itself absurd.

Happily, the restored version will live in the hearts and memories of film fans and historians, and also in the history of science fiction.

The significance of this motion picture to science fiction buffs (or "Slans") like myself cannot be overstated. Those pathetic creatures, no doubt produced by parallel evolution, who happen to share our planet, known as non-science fiction buffs (or "Muggles") join us in appreciating this strange and monumental masterpiece. The endless war between Slans, who live in basements and eat burritos, and

Muggles, who have jobs and girlfriends, is suspended for a season when we join in shared admiration for this movie.

Slans and Muggles must live together. They must come home from their jobs and we must come up from our basements and shake hands and live in brother-love forever. *Between the slans and the muggles the heart must mediate.*

3

MY INVASIONS PLANS

*THE QUESTION in bold was asked of several authors on a website
called SF Brain Parade. My answer follows:*

**We apologize for the inconvenience, but the planet
Earth is scheduled for alien invasion. Your species' custom
is important to us. Please leave a message at the tone indi-
cating your preferred choice of alien invader and why.**

1. The aliens we *most* want to be invaded by are, of course,
the organ-harvesting, poison-gas-spewing gray aliens from
M. Night Shyamalan's *Signs*. This is for several reasons. First,
they seem unable to organize an actual military occupation:
they merely raid and leave. Second, they have a fatal weakness to a substance commonly found in abundance on our
planet, which makes their invasion of us about as absurd as
Earthmen invading Venus, whose atmosphere is mostly
sulfuric acid. Third, their weakness would have been entirely
nonoperative against them, had they remembered to wear
their space armor, or, for that matter, their Mackintoshes
and galoshes. It is to be devoutly hoped that we are invaded

by such galactic ninnies: they are not smart enough to come in out of the rain.

2. The Martians of H.G. Wells are much more efficient and ruthless, of course, but they land on a world and feast on the blood of the inhabitants by injecting it into their own veins, without first checking for disease-bearing microbes, or, for that matter, peanut intolerance. One might excuse this oversight on the grounds that they long ago eliminated pathogens on their world, making deadly viruses as extinct as the dodo. On the other hand, no one goes to another world without quarantine procedures. So the Martians are ninnies also, and we could hold them off for a week or so, while they caught the sniffles and died. While their heat rays and black smoke might pose a problem for unarmed civilians, a fleet of ships like the HMS Thunderchild are clearly their match; or we could just shovel dirt over their shells when they landed, since they sit in a crater bottom for a day or three recovering from the shock of being fired by cannon from Mars.

3. The organ-harvesting aliens from Sylvia and Gerry Anderson's *UFO* are next. While they occasionally can do effective acts of sabotage, such as making a human being into a time bomb or giving them evil ESP, the threat they pose is so minimal, that their raids into Earth space do not even come to the attention of the people of Earth. The Earth population during wartime is not making the sacrifices and enduring the hardships of London in the Blitz; they are not even enduring the fears of civilians in the Cold War. The UFO Menace is so slight, that they can be fended off by a secret organization with fewer members than an average aircraft carrier: SHADO has one moonbase with three good-looking WACs in purple wigs, three space-craft that shoot one missile each, three aircraft, a halftrack and a submarine. Meanwhile, the UFO men are from a dying planet, which

means each attack will be weaker and more desperate than the last. Southern France is more likely to conquer the world than the green-liquid- breathers.

4. Much more menacing are the aliens from *Independence Day*. Unlike the goofballs mentioned above, they actually have a military organization, large-scale ships, firepower, and pose a real threat. However, their electronic counter-intelligence is not as sophisticated as my Norton Firewall I bought for my laptop, so maybe we do not need to worry about their superior alien intelligence either. Dorks.

5. The Martians from *Mars Attacks* can be done in with Country Music. I would not normally mention this during an interview by a serious SF Brain Parade asking a serious SF question to a serious SF author about our very, very serious genre, which is all about Space Pirates kidnapping Space Princesses, except that an invasion by these Martians would allow the Dixie Chicks, by playing *Cowboy Take Me Away* at high volume to emerge as truly patriotic heroines, and mollifying their flyover-country audiences.

6. One of the more serious movies in our serious genre is, of course, *Queen of Outer Space*, starring Zsa Zsa Gabor. The invasion here would consist of a single shot from a femm-ray cannon that would wipe out our planet instantly, so you would think I would not request to be invaded by the Venusians. However, Zsa Zsa, when she was young, had quite an appealing feminine mystique (she waz built like da Brick House!), and in order to overcome this particular threat, all we need do is offer the Evil Queen some quick plastic surgery and Brad Pitt or Orlando Bloom, and we are set. The Venusians all wear short skirts and high heels and they have showgirl legs, so, even if we lose the war, it can't be all that bad.

7. Invasion by the Ferengi of *Star Trek: The Next Generation* is next on my request list of wimpy, dorky invaders. The

super evil evilness of the Ferengi consists of the fact that they are (gasp of horror, please) Yankee Traders. (This phrase is used twice by Lt. Data when they are first introduced). Getting Ferengied by the Ferengi is about like being robbed by a Robber Baron: in other words, a guy comes up to you and sells you something you want, like oil, steel, or computer software. He does it again and again until your economy is humming, and you are rich. Then you complain about what a bum he is. It is true that they might try to sell you shabby goods. Caveat emptor.

8. Invasion by the *Predators* is my next request. They have no military organization, and only form big-game hunting parties. In other words, they are Count Zaroff from Space. As far as I can tell, they are as completely honorable as Barsoomians, and will holster their fire-arms if their prey does not have a fire-arm, and they will not kill pregnant game. We can defeat them easily with our current military, merely by having our Navy servicewomen go out on long cruises with all the lusty young sailors in our fleet, and then, when they have a bun in the oven, muster out and shoot the Rastas From Space, who will not shoot back. Our girls in uniform are pretty badass, and could probably hand them their yarbles with not much effort.

9. Invasion by the Peacekeepers of *Farscape* is my next request. Now, the Peacekeepers, unlike all the other goons and slobs listed above, are actually squared away, so being defeated by them in no dishonor to us. It is like being creamed by the Spartans. Even if you lose, no one will point and laugh at you, unlike if you lose to, say, Ewoks. (Boy, I'd hate to be a Stormtrooper from that unit back the barracks, trying to explain how my tank was put out of commission by a teddy bear armed with lumber.) But we might not lose to the Peacekeepers, since all we have to do is fight them in the desert, until they faint from the heat.

10. The last invader, the one I do not want to be invaded by, is the most sinister and powerful of all. You might guess that I mean Ming of Mongo, who is the most tyrannical of all space tyrants, and who likes to play with planets before destruction. While I fear him (and who does not?) there is one invader I fear more. I mean the psychohistorians from *Foundation*. They will not fire a shot. We will not even be aware of the war. They will land an agent or two, maybe publish a book, maybe organize a trade union or an election campaign, maybe influence a thought or two with their brain powers, and then depart. Math does the rest. We will stare in bewilderment as riots and changes in demographics, unexpected movements of immigration or sudden shifts in the economy, and we will see no one and nothing to fight. Then, one day, with the inevitability of mathematics, ships land with their Spaceship-and-Sun emblems of the Second Galactic Empire emblazoned on their hulls, and we willingly or unwillingly (doesn't matter what we do, the result is the same) join and vow loyalty to Trantor. Now, if you have to get conquered, and there is no way out, these Psychohistorians are the guys you want to have to conquer you. First, joining the empire ensures peace and stability and, best of all, trade. You can sell earth-goods all the way to Terminus without worrying about Space Pirates. Second, no one fires a shot, no death camps, no torture amplifiers, no man-eating lizard-men. The only drawback is a complete and horrifying loss of freedom and democracy. No one votes for a psychohistorian any more than they vote for a jedi.

As a thought-experiment, let us assume the invaders land in order, and see what would result:

1. *Signs* aliens land in the rain, and die.

2. *War* of the Worlds Martians land in the rain, get a cold, and die.

3.*UFO* aliens blown out of the sky by secret organization, and die.

4. *Independence Day* aliens blow up White House, Empire State Building, and Mount Rushmore, but a fourteen-year-old hacker opens up their Force Shield, and a drunk pilot kamekazes into the mothership. They die, we get their equipment and reverse engineer it.

5. *Mars Attacks* Martians land, but after invasion #4, we nuke them before they get the hatches open. Or play Dixie Chicks.

6. Lonely good-looking girls from Venus attack. Maybe we can put up the force screen we reverse-engineered from invasion #4, and survive the Femm-ray long enough to apologize, sweet talk the little gals, and make some time.

7. Ferengi invade and… it is like having Standard Oil, US Steel, and Microsoft offer you a new range of products. We get rich, so we can buy the good-looking alien babes from invasion #6 a diamond ring or mink coat.

8. Predators come. By this time the good-looking alien babes are happily married and well-armed, which means the Predators are bound by honor code not to kill them, so the well-armed and pregnant showgirls can kill off the Predators with their femm-rays.

9. Peacekeepers. Fight them in the Sahara, that is our only hope. Unlike all the other invaders, they are not nincompoops, so we probably lose this one rather badly. The only advantage: interfertile. Humans are badass enough that, despite our weak eyes, we may be allowed to join the Sebacean military and serve as auxiliaries.

10. Psychohistorians. It does not matter what the Sebaceans do, or the good-looking alien showgirls from Venus, or Supergirl from plant Krypton (or Argo, if you insist). The Earth-Conquering Peacekeepers will be overwhelmed by the forces of history, and will join up (willingly

or not, it does not matter) with the Second Galactic Empire, and now Earth has two layers of rulership. Game over. The good thing about Psychohistory is, of course, from now on you can rest assured that all wars and economic depressions have been accounted for in Seldon's Plan, so if your planet suffers, it will hereafter be for the greater good of the Empire. And the Second Empire, by exterminating the Predators and protecting the trade routes of the Ferengi, might allow the dying worlds of Mars, *UFO*, *Signs* and *Independence Day*, to revive themselves or migrate.

4

REVIEW OF THE MOVIE WE'VE ALL BEEN WAITING FOR

LIKE MANY PEOPLE, when I heard the news that the Disney corporation had purchased the rights to make Star Wars sequels, I feared they might gut the heart of the series, fumble even basic storytelling principles, and insult the viewers with Mary Sue heroines, diversity hire characters, tangled yet aimless plots, deconstruction and desecration of the original fan-favorite heroes, all topped off with heavy-handed political posturing crammed down the throat of the audience, mangling and mutating the most beloved franchise in movie history into a putrid and unsightly sewer fire.

I am glad to report that I need not have fretted. Two films of the new trilogy are out, and the filmmakers avoided all these pitfalls and pratfalls.

The twin errors any sequel in any genre must avoid are these: first, the sequel must not violate or overturn anything established in the original, including taking care to continue with themes, story elements, characters and backdrops the audience expects; second, the sequel must not cling too closely to the original, nor be content merely to repeat story elements.

You cannot simply have the rebels still fighting the self-same Empire they defeated in the last movie blowing up yet another iteration of the Death Star. That would be ridiculous! Luckily, they didn't do that!

It is something of a paradox, since the audience wants the same story that they liked the first time, but not done in the same way.

The cleverest and most satisfying way I have ever seen a writer answer this paradox was E.E. Doc Smith, when he opened *Gray Lensman* with the startling revelation that the villainous space pirate king, Helmuth, slain in climactic combat at the end of *Galactic Patrol*, was himself merely an agent of a larger, deeper, darker group.

Now, of course, this tradition is not new to EE Smith. Beowulf, after slaying Grendel in the golden hall of Hereot, is permitted no long rest, but must descend into an accursed swamp to fight Grendel's Mother, a monstrous hag tougher than the first monster.

In this way, the hero, or the hero's heirs or disciples, is, in effect, fighting for the same cause and against the same foe, but the significance of the first victory is not diminished. Instead, the scope is larger, and the battlefield gets bigger.

How to make something as huge and simple as an evil Galactic Empire merely the outward sign of a deeper hidden power is a question to stump most writers, but I think the filmmaker here answered this cleverly, and in a way in keeping with everything the canon had established.

Let me give a scene by scene review. I hope I can be forgiven for giving such a long and in-depth description, but this film was so remarkable, and the mistakes that could have been made were so neatly avoided, I think it worth the time to ponder how well the Disney writers treated the franchise. Remember how worried we were that it would just be a piece of leftwingnut feminist crud?

EPISODE SEVEN: THE DARK SIDE RISING

*The Dark Side Rising*in the opening word crawl announces that Luke Skywalker has vanished. The young and untried Jedi graduating from his new Academy are scouring the galaxy, searching for him. However, there is one place no searcher dares to go: the mysterious Black Sun Nebula surrounding the supermassive black hole at the core of the galaxy. One by one, the core stars are going out, leaving whole planets to freeze in darkness. And the nebula is spreading.

One young Jedi, hunted by sinister agents of the power behind the Empire, holds the sole clue to the secret of the dying stars...

I thought it was cool that, as the word crawl was done crawling, the stars were going out, one by one. Then the camera zooms in on one emerald-green planet, Ambria.

We are quickly introduced to the heroine of the film, as well as the heavy. We meet young Lyra Sentara in flashback.

She is orphaned when the sun of her home world of Ambria flickers and fades like a dying candle, snow fills the air, and maddened mobs rush to seize any starship to be found, including her father's one-man fighter parked on the roof of the Jedi Temple. Her father, lightsaber in hand, fends off the panicked crowd on the narrow and un-railed bridge leading to the launch pad. Explosions throw the screaming refugees off to either side, and Imperial Stormtroopers close in on the father. The father draws his lightsaber. The lead stormtrooper flourishes a weapon that looks like a cross between like a two-forked trident and a Jacob's ladder (I am sure they got the design from Matt Wagner's *Grendel*, if any of you are old enough to remember that). The father blasts the stormtrooper with a gush of red lightning right in the face.

The mother sacrifices her life getting Lyra to the one-man ship, cut down from behind. The scene is all the more effective because there is no dialog: only the sound effects, and the stirring music.

The scene where the stormtrooper captain yanks off his burnt and scarred helmet to show his burnt and scarred face beneath, and glare with his remaining good eye at the fleeing X-wing just as the sun flickers and goes out is the one you saw in all the trailers.

Now, I realize continuity mavens will object that all the stormtroopers are clones of Jango Fett, and therefore one could not be a black man, but since the black man, in this case, is Will Smith playing a bad-ass bad guy, I, for one, do not mind.

It is not as if the film makers put in a Black Stormtrooper and then just make him an incompetent cowardly boob easily beaten up by a female half his size. Also, when Smith's character Captain Keyel Ansteel [SPOILERS!] does an about-face and works for the good guys [as if anyone expected Will Smith to remain a bad guy the whole trilogy], he does not become a good man. He is still a battle-scarred killer, cold and remorseless and totally hard-core.

Frankly, I thought the idea of having a stormtrooper defect to the Republic was simply brilliant. Previous movies merely assumed that the viewer would assume any empire was a bad thing, and any rebellion a good thing. What life in an Orwellian totalitarianism was like was not on stage. In fact, I was a little surprised that, in this day and age of political correctness, we would have a scene where a grown man finds out that he has been lied to his whole life on the screen. Most likely the filmmakers did not realize what a sharp criticism it was of political correctness to have the ex-stormtrooper taken to a bazaar, and simply to see the lavish amounts of goods for sale, the children laughing and playing, men and women talking and walking freely.

More haunting is the scene where he looks at a star map, and we find out, for the first time in his life, that the stormtroopers are raised from birth believing that all the stars in the galaxy, all the planets he has never visited, are still loyal to the Empire. The stormtroopers are told that there is no republic: only a few scattered and discontented planets engaged in a futile rebellion.

Like many viewers, I do not mind a racially mixed cast, as long as it is done to help the movie tell a good story, and not done merely to score boasting rights for would-be social justice warriors pretending to battle prejudices that died out over half a century ago. The decision to have the main character of *Dark Side Rising* be an oriental female did not strike me as being particularly boast-worthy, not in these days, but I am glad the girl was not some Mary Sue to whom everything is easy, and everyone loves, as far, far too many modern female characters are portrayed.

I am also glad that the rumors that the oriental actress portraying Lyra was not a "body-positive" "healthy at any size" ugly and chubby girl turned out to be false. The Chinese have an eye for beauty, and nearly all Chinese actresses in their films these days are drop-dead gorgeous. So, it was very pleasing to me that the actress here was one whose name I recognized: Tiffany Tang (Tang Yan).

Also, the complaint that we saw the Mom hand the sacred scroll to the robot, that later changed into a space map, is false. The thing the Mom is bending over to place in the robot is the space map. I am not sure why anyone is confused on this point.

Now grown-up Lyra wakes in a panic sweat, remembering her dreadful childhood. Red force-lightning crackles on her fingers and in her eyes, until she can meditate and calm her anger. Then she opens one eye, and looks around, as if trying to tell if anyone noticed.

We discover she is one of the few remaining students of the Jedi Academy on planet Ossus, a poisoned planet of vapors overgrown with deadly fungi and giant mushrooms. The domed temple of the Jedi looms above an empty, deserted city. The temple itself is almost empty, since most of the students are on the quest.

Lyra says her farewells to those who have taken up the quest. As their ships depart, we see sinister ships hidden in the ring system circling the planet. Robots wake pilots and assassins from suspended animation, saying that the place must be almost deserted by now. Dark ships with quiet engines follow a shower of meteors down through the atmosphere, undetected.

Lyra goes to the Headmistress of the Jedi Academy, Luminara Unduli, and reports her dream, and says she now remembers more of what happened on that day. Stormtroopers did indeed kill her parents nine years ago. Luminara says, no, the Empire was defeated twenty years ago, and is no longer a threat. Lyra retorts that the Empire does still exist and must be the power behind the Black Sun Nebula.

Rumors persist that the Admirals of the Imperial Starfleet, driven off but not driven to surrender, have soldiers, ships, and materiel hidden among the uncharted pirate planets beyond the edge of the galaxy. Luminara says the once-proud imperial stormtroopers, if any still live, have been reduced to being mere space pirates, preying on random, unarmed freighters at the edge of the galaxy, and are no threat to anyone here.

I got to say, I love the idea of pirate planets.

Lyra has spent months scouring the Jedi Library, and has found many references to one sacred scroll describing the source of the Dark Side, naming the legendary figure that started the Sith Order, and telling of an ancient, mystical artifact called the Great Eye of Darkness. Vader once boasted that the Death Star's power as was nothing compared to the power of the Force: the Great Eye might have been what he had in mind. But she can find no trace of the sacred scroll itself. She is convinced her father had found the sole surviving copy.

Lyra and Luminara journey to the Library of the Jedi, which is housed in a great tree in the midst of a garden, beneath a huge dome. It looks like something out of a Miyazaki movie. Luminara tells how Master Ood Bnar, a thousand years ago, transfigured himself into an immobile, treelike being, growing over, around, and into the library, in order to protect it. The scrolls, books, tapes and datafiles had been scattered during the Imperial times, but the tree was intact, if damaged, and Ood's memory remained impregnated in the bark long after his death. The tree itself remembered each book that had been lost, for each shelf and cubby in the library was carved out of his living substance.

If the sacred scroll was indeed a missing treasure of the Jedi lore lost during the Imperial years, the tree would know it was missing.

Lyra places her hands on the tree trunk and talks to it using the jedi-mindspeech. The voice of Ood, or his blue-lit ghost, appears, and assures her that the sacred scroll her father was guarding was not any part of the Jedi library nor lore. There is no scroll missing. All have been recovered.

Luminara makes the point that the plants (the glow-in-the-dark floaty puffballs taken straight from James Cameron's *Avatar*) here in this garden are the only surviving descendants of the original ecosystem of Ossus, and that the Jedi are replanting the seeds outside, regrowing the survivors, aiding and nurturing the healthy growth, in the hope that one day the biological weapons, mold and fungi, introduced by the Evil Empire overwhelming the planet outside will fail.

The metaphor was obvious, and Lyra gets it, and agrees to stay and concentrate on her training.

Even though it is brief, we a get a clear description of the difference between the Force and the Dark Side. The Force is a field of positive energy flowing between and through all life in the galaxy: when an organism turns to fear, hatred, aggression, falsehood, the force is disturbed and out of balance. It creates a snarl, a shadow, as a rock in a stream creates a back eddy.

During all this, Lyra realizes that Luminara is keeping her here to protect her. From whom? From what? If the Empire is dead, what is the threat? Luminara says cryptically that there are "Phantoms of the Empire—even when dead, there are some things that cannot die."

But there is also a pretty clear implication that Luminara is afraid of Lyra turning to the Dark Side.

Just then, the sun starts flickering. It suddenly gets very dark.

The filmmaker evidently believes the old rule of thumb that any story is better if you add ninjas. The argument between Luminara and Lyra is interrupted when thin and creepy looking aliens in black camouflage crawl up the side of the tower. Much has been written about the space ninjas, and you saw them on the teaser trailer, so let me just say they were visually dramatic. The fight scene between the over-matched Jedi students and the cyborg space ninja in the burning Jedi Temple is a classic. I particularly liked when the Ood tree came to life and used its branches to punt people.

Like everyone, I was sorry when the Jedi Library tree was burnt down to a stub. Burning books, especially burning holy books containing thousands of years of painfully accu-mulated lore and wisdom, is about the most vile thing I can think of, and the filmmaker thought so too. At that point, there is nothing else the viewer needs to see or know about the book-burners to know they are irredeemably evil.

Some reviewers did not understand that the atmosphere is not poisonous, but the spores that come in when the dome is broken are poisonous, which is why Luminara can survive with just a scarf over her face. The scene where she dies, I thought she was dying of wounds from the laser-throwing-star thingies the space ninjas throw, not that she was choking.

Luminara is dying and tells Lyra to go find Luke Skywalker. He alone, if anyone can, will discover the reason behind the Black Sun Nebula. But she warns Lyra to be mindful of herself, to avoid wrath and pride, because there is a darkness in her past, and a darkness in her destiny.

Lyra demands "What past? My father was a great Jedi!"

"He was something else..." But Luminara passes away and vanishes before she can explain more. (Not to worry: she just fainted. She gets better, and comes back in the last reel).

Lyra is captured, but saves herself when red lightning bursts from her eyes and mouth, and she cuts down her captor.

She then kills the TIE fighter pilot and puts on his uniform and helmet. As she is leaving the planet in her captor's captured ship, she sees the true size of the space pirate fleet. The ring system circling the planet (the astronomic knowledge-free filmmakers call it an "asteroid belt") had ships behind every boulder in space.

She joins the fleet and leaves the system. The Jedi Temple on Ossus burns behind her, the only point of light on a sunless planet.

Lyra radios that she has engine trouble, saying she has to halt for repairs. The fleet captain is suspicious, but is apparently vulnerable to a Jedi mind trick even over the radio. She drops out of the black fleet formation, lags behind, and makes a break for it.

As the camera pans back, we see an X-wing, with the familiar dome of R2D2 protruding from the hull, following the black fleet at a distance.

Lyra discovers the navigation pod is locked. Only the origin and destination stars are visible. Every other part of the map is blacked out. She has to navigate by dead reckoning and dumb luck.

After the defeat of the Imperial starfleet, Queen Leia and General Solo have retired to a life of peace on the rural prairie planet Dungreen, content to let a younger generation guide the fledgling Republic.

Lyra flies to the golden planet Dungreen, lands, and after some silly rigmarole involving giant prairie dogs, is rescued by Chewbacca the Wookie. He leads her to the sprawling royal hacienda, which is dug into a wide pit just below the level of the endless grassland, and so is invisible from even a few yards away to someone approaching on foot. It is a cool visual.

(Why Lyra did not see it from the air is a nitpick viewers with too much time on their hands have argued about. I love being a Star Wars fan. We nitpick and argue about everything.)

The actors are a little long in the tooth, and I understand that Carrie Fisher passed away after most the primary filming was done, but not all. May she rest in peace. Some of the scenes of Queen Leia surrounded by her children and grandchildren in their huge hacienda were done with clever computer graphics. Some people complained they looked fake or had the uncanny valley effect: my eye was fooled. I could spot no difference between CGI Leia and real Leia.

And, of course, General Solo still has the Millennium Falcon in his garage, that he tinkers with and overhauls, even if he has twenty other prettier and new space yachts all bright and shiny right next door. "This old girl still has some fight in her," he says.

We get to meet their younger kids, Ben Solo, the twins Jaina and Jacen Solo, and little Anakin. In the Expanded Universe books (which I have not had the pleasure of reading) I believe one of them ends up as a Sith Dark Lord named Darth Caedus. I am glad the movie makers did not go with this. The idea that Han and Leia would have anything other than a long and happy marriage with well-raised and happy children would betray the fairytale flavor and concept of the whole *Star Wars* universe.

Chewbacca, in subtitles, explains that in his 400 years of life, he has taken to keeping and breeding Solos. Den Solo, Jonash Solo, Han Solo, and now the younger generation are like his pets: they are rascally critters, and he has to keep them out of trouble.

Some of the fans do not like the scene where Leia dresses down Lyra, but I thought it was fine. At the time, I also wondered by Lyra, disguised in one of the enemy TIE fighters, did not simply follow along with the fleet and find their secret base. Lyra is told she is too young and inexperienced. But Lyra thinks Queen Leia's objection has more to do with whatever the "dark destiny" hanging over her is. She thinks the queen is afraid of her.

Lyra says the Empire is real, and they are the ones extinguishing suns. Leia says that such a thing is impossible: no known technology, no known science, could explain how to kill a sun. Only the Sith, with their command of the force, could do such a thing: but they are all dead.

Queen Leia insists that the raid on Ossus must have been conducted by space pirates, merely villainous scum, and that the organization and morale of the Empire was shattered decades ago. There is no more Empire.

Why would the Empire, if it still existed and was still a power to be feared, attack what amounted to an empty building with a few teachers and children in it?

Moreover, the police have impounded Lyra's stolen pirate ship, because they want to examine it for clues, and to decrypt the navigation pod. Lyra is thanked, but told the space police and star navy will handle the pirate threat from now on, and seek out the pirates who raided Ossus.

Lyra sits brooding, red sparks dancing in her eyes, trying to control herself.

Now we cut back to the black fleet. We see the secret planet of the space pirates: a barren and airless landscape of craters. And then we see a hatch open between two mountains, and the fleet enters a hollow world with an artificial sun at that center.

Scientifically, of course, it makes no sense at all (all points inside a sphere whose skin layer is equal mass in all directions would suffer zero gravity). But visually, having oceans and farmlands and mountains and cities clinging to the inside of a vast sphere is cool. It is a quick way of showing the audience that the Empire has entire worlds and industrial cities at their command, of which the Republic knows nothing, and cannot detect from space.

We meet Captain Ansteel again. (Will Smith in an eyepatch). He is reporting to a sober-looking six-year-old boy, who is apparently the Emperor. Grand Admiral Thrawn, a blue-face Kalonian, tells the Emperor to go play, and hears the report. The sacred scroll was not found. The daughter of Sentara was not found. They were not on Ossus.

(How the kid could be six, if the death of Palpatine at Endor was twenty years ago, is not explained. Maybe he is a clone. Or maybe he is a nephew. Or his species ages slowly.)

Thrawn speaks to two scientists, asking them how long until the Great Eye of Darkness will be restored, and ready to use again. The scientists explain the artifact is very old, and only the sacred scroll contains all the secrets of its construction. One of them says, "If, perhaps, if one of these young Jedi students were allowed to examine it, he could tell us things our instruments cannot." Thrawn dismisses them angrily.

Captain Ansteel says that some of the students captured at the academy are younglings, little more than children. "If they were trained properly... if they could be *turned* to the Dark Side..."

Thrawn says, "The loyalty of Dark Jedi is never complete. They are not Sith. They never will be. No Sith can turn to Jedi, not completely. No Jedi serving the Dark Side can be trusted, even after years of loyalty. Remember the treason of Lord Vader! It is your turn to babysit the Emperor."

Thrawn then speaks to an unseen personage, promising that the Great Eye of Darkness will be up and running again soon, and that it will not be long now until the Republic...er, Rebellion...will fall, once and for all.

The students we saw captured by the space ninja are brought out into an arena. Little Jedi kids are thrown to the Sarlac and eaten alive. Ansteel is stonyfaced, standing next to the throne, as the six-year-old Emperor laughs and claps.

We see a mysterious robed man watching Ansteel. Ansteel flinches, and turns, scanning the crowd, knowing he is being watched.

Then back to Lyra. Why Chewie decides to steal the Millennium Falcon, and go flipping off into space with her, is not really made clear. I assume the filmmaker just wanted the iconic ship back on screen, and this was the easiest way to do it.

Lyra and Chewie fly to Coruscant, the capital. The spaceport is crowded with throngs of refugees fleeing from solar systems whose suns have died.

There is a brief montage of Lyra trying to talk to various bureaucrats and naval officers, and being given the brush off. Lyra says she knows where the secret of how the Empire is killing suns is hidden: her old home planet, Ambria. But this is in the Black Sun Nebula at the core of the galaxy, and too many ships and outposts near there have been mysteriously lost, and so it is unsafe to travel there. No one is allowed to go for any reason.

She sits by a fountain in a park, head in her hands, beneath three statues (poised in the iconic posture similar to the old movie poster) of young Leia, Luke and Han as heroes of the New Republic. Lyra tells the statues that they were lucky: the Death Star was a large and obvious threat. But when the enemy is a phantom no one can find, how can anyone fight it?

Chewie indicates that he has an idea. He leads her to the vast and grand Senate building, and finds a small and unguarded door in a narrow back alley nearby. Chewie says Han Solo's eldest son works in this building.

We now meet Napoleon Solo. He is leaning in a chair, his feet up on a desk, tossing a rubber ball against the far wall. A robotic mop is swabbing the floor. Lyra says to Chewie, "I thought you said he worked in the Senate."

Naps says, "I work in the building. I am a janitor. I clean up messes."

Lyra, "But this is a senator's office. And I thought only robots did janitorial work?"

"This senator in particular makes messes. I supervise the clean-up robots." He bounces his rubber ball off the automatic mop, which beeps loudly at him. "You missed a spot."

Lyra explains her quest: she believes her frozen home-world of Ambria holds the sacred scroll where the secret weapon being used by the Empire to extinguish suns is described. But Ambria is inside the spreading effect of the Black Sun Nebula, and to journey there is forbidden.

Naps hops out of the chair. He says that as a member of the Senatorial staff, he has a pass to allow him where other citizens are not allowed to go. He says "C'mon! I could use a vacation."

He opens a closet, and we see robot duplicate of him: Robo Solo. Robo Solo is told to hold down the fort and clean up the messes while Naps is gone.

Lyra goggles. "You have your own robot duplicate to do your janitorial work for you?"

Naps grins. "My Mom is a Queen. Rank hath its privileges, don't you know."

Aboard the Millennium Falcon, Chewie, Lyra, and Naps head toward the dark core of the galaxy.

Meanwhile, back at the hollow pirate planet, Kaas, Captain Ansteel travels to the barren surface. He stands in the middle of a flat plane of black glass, draws his blaster rifle, and waits. After a while, the mysterious robed figure is seen walking slowly across the black surface toward him. Ansteel shoots: the blaster bolt sizzles through the air. The robed man raises a hand. The bolt slows, and halts, frozen in midmotion. The man walks past it, whereupon the blast leaps into motion, striking the ground. The gust of wind throws the man's hood aside. It is Luke Skywalker, now a fierce-looking old man, battle-scarred and bearded.

Luke says: "There is a better way."

Ansteel says: "Empire requires iron discipline, yes, and even cruelty. It is bad, but the alternative is worse. Whenever one rebellion is squelched, another rises. So it has been my whole life. So it will be for all eternity."

Luke: "There is always the third option, Flint."

Ansteel: "Wait. How do you know my birth name? I have been KL-NSTL since I was taken from my parents! They were traitors. My whole life has been spent in service to the empire, attempting to expiate that stain!"

"They were heroes. They would have wished for something better."

"Better, how? Either there will be lawlessness and destruction, or there will peace beneath the iron boot of the Empire."

"The Republic might win, and bring peace and freedom to the entire galaxy."

Ansteel, looking confused: "The Republic? What's that?"

Luke offers to show him. They board Ansteel's runabout, and fly off.

Meanwhile, aboard the Millennium Falcon, as they approach the dead star of Ambria, they run into pirate ships with big skull and crossbones emblazoned on their hulls. A fight ensues. When the Falcon's guns cuts one of the smaller ships in half, the skull and crossbones falls away, revealing the imperial cogwheel beneath. Tractor beams grapple the Falcon, and stormtroopers jetpack across the space between, clamping to the hull with magnetic shoes and unlimbering cutting tools to get through the hull.

The difference between modern special effects and the 1970s effects is well on display in the fight scene in zero gravity while the wounded Falcon is suffering hurricanic winds due to explosive decompression. This was filmed in a soundstage built in the belly of a Boeing Stratotanker. Now, I realize that in real life, wearing nothing but a little mask over your mouth and nose would not protect an astronaut from zero air pressure, and no one can possibly, just by holding a hand-hold, pull himself up against decompression winds blowing at fifteen pounds per square inch, but maybe unseen gravity rays were keeping part of the air back, or protecting the crew, or maybe the Force was with them. Whatever. It was cool looking.

Captain Ansteel's ship arrives on the scene, and he orders the pirates to stand down. They defy him. He opens fire.

Luke then shows his awesome power, what a Jedi can really do, when he floats into the space between the ships, deflects or parries the full barrage of a warship. As he concentrates, switches onboard the enemy ship flips themselves, red lights light up and sirens wail, and *kaboom*.

A lot of people complained that this was more power than the Jedi were ever shown to use before. Maybe. But having a Jedi float around in outer space without a suit I suppose could be possible for a man with lifelong training. It is not as if the movie is asking us to believe, for example, that an untrained elderly politician whose brother merely happened to be a Jedi could pull off a stunt like that.

Luke floats in through the broken hull of the Millennium Falcon. He sternly asks Lyra why she is not studying at her classes at the Academy, and she, even more sternly asks him why, he is not teaching her classes at the academy.

Luke says that his visions of the future grew darker, and vanished entirely. Only one order ever learned how to use the Dark Side of the Force to cloak their actions, so that even Jedi could not see, feel, or sense their hidden moves. As the sole remaining Jedi Master in the galaxy, it was his duty, his alone, to seek out the source of the dark power.

Untrained Jedi, those who had never touched true evil, and who had no understanding of how seductive the Dark Side could be, would be in greater danger than someone with no training at all.

Lyra demands to know what he fears. Luke will not say.

It cannot be the Sith! Lyra says that the Sith are dead. Vader and Palpatine were the last of them. The dead cannot harm the living.

Luke says that we can never leave the past behind: the dead inspire the living and guide us. It was Obi-Wan Kenobi's guidance, after he was dead, which destroyed the Death Star.

Ansteel takes the wounded ship in tow.

They reach Ambria. The sunless world is coated with ice, and cities and still-preserved corpses in postures of panic are trapped in the frozen atmosphere.

In special toyetic cold suits, they walk until the reach the spot under which the old Jedi Temple is buried: and they come across an excavation pit. Some unknown party had gone to great lengths to burrow down into the frozen ice, hauled it away, and carefully cleared the buildings of ice, digging everything free.

Lyra follows one of these tunnels driven through the ice of frozen atmosphere, and walks into her old house. She goes through the kitchen and bedchamber (which we saw briefly in the opening scene.) Recovered rubbish, flotsam and jetsam is neatly stored and numbered and piled in what once was the spaceport, each piece inside its own block of ice. All is surrounded by spidery black lamps. Some crew had been doing archeological work here, digging carefully, looking for something.

Lyra looks at the frozen rubbish. She sees her old Ewok doll and other toys. The ball-shaped BB-8 droid is there in its own icecube. She rests her hand thoughtfully on it for a moment. Someone calls. She turns to go.

After she leaves, we see the droid stir to life. Its lenses and status lights light up. A whirring blade comes out of a slot. The little droid begins to cut itself free.

One of the tunnels through the ice leads into the Jedi Temple. They reach the door of the temple, but find it locked. The spidery lamps lining the ice tunnel turn out to be droids who had been standing still. They unfold into long insectoid killer-droids, and emit blaster bolts from their lighting fixtures as they stalk forward. The group is trapped in a narrow tunnel leading to a locked door.

Just as all is lost, BB-8 opens the door from the inside, revealing a conveniently placed giant gun. He makes a comical beeping and opens fire. The fighting droids are blasted into smithereens.

It turns out that BB-8 does not have the sacred scroll. But he does have Lyra's father's research and records, including an ancient star map, thousands of generations old. The map is so old that the stars are in different positions than are marked here, and different stellar types. The hidden location of the sacred scroll is at a star which is a black sun that appears on no map known to civilization. Lyra's father calculated its current location from its orbit around the center of the galaxy (and I am sorry for the fanboys who complained that this was a gaffe, and that stars did not have orbits—this part is scientifically accurate).

It is labeled as Nastrond, the homeworld of the Sith. It is currently inside the Black Sun Nebula.

There is a scene where they land on a planet Takodana to get Millennium Falcon repaired. Ansteel goes sightseeing with Luke, and he learns what life in the Republic is like. He sees a map for the first time, and discovers that the Black Sun Nebula, which he thought covered the entire galaxy, is only the small volume of space near the core.

I thought this scene was awkwardly placed, considering we were in the last reel, but at this point it was also clear to me that the filmmakers were not going to resolve all their ongoing plotlines in one movie.

Nonetheless, I really like the bit where we find out how much the dwindling remnant of the Empire (which still includes scores of planets) lies to the stormtroopers. Flint had no idea that the many rebellions he had fought over the years were part of one organized effort, or that his enemies had won some of the battles. The Empire tells its subjects and troopers that every time a battalion withdraws from battle, that another battalion actually won that skirmish. Flint had been raised to know of nothing but a string of uninterrupted victories in a galaxy he thought was nearly all loyal planets. Instead his whole civilization is nothing but a few pirates clinging to scattered bases either in a dark area near the core where no one goes, or planets hidden in small star clusters outside the main disk of the galaxy.

Flint says his ship is a pirate ship, and will attract attention. He moves his gear aboard the Millennium Falcon, including a mysterious black box which, when his back is turned, unfolds an antenna and starts beeping.

The Millennium falcon and the black runabout are met by a Republican blockade when they try to enter the Black Sun Nebula: Naps beams his credentials across to the picket ships, but the officers say that their ship is reported as stolen. Naps groans and mutters "Mo-om!" But then he grins, and over Lyra's objection, he dives into a nearby convenient asteroid swarm, dodges flying rocks, and leads the picket ships in a merry chase, and dumps flares, blows up an asteroid behind him, ejecting prepackaged debris as he does so, and then sneaks away, clinging to an asteroid going deeper into the Nebula.

They arrive at Nastrond. The planet has no sun, but, somehow, the atmosphere is heated and the surface is habitable. Chains of volcanos and oceans of surface lava cover the surface.

They land at the designated spot. The mountain ranges, like evil versions of Mount Rushmore, have all been carved into devil faces and skull faces. On an island in the middle of a lake of lava, connected by thin and unrailed bridges to the many-windowed cliffs all around, is a flat-topped red dome. A ring of parabolic dishes surrounds the crown.

Cautiously, they land, cross the bridge above the lava, and enter the dome.

The inside of the dome, in all its ruby and gold magnificence, is revealed to their eyes. Gothic caryatids of skeletal, bat-winged figures hold up a vast dome. A giant crystal hangs in mid-air above a glowing red pit.

Everyone looks awed but Luke. "This is a temple" he says. A Jedi Temple? "No. A Sith Temple." He points at the giant crystal, and says it is a lightsaber crystal, focusing an immense amount of the Force in this chamber, but distorting it, staining it, snarling it.

On an altar beneath the crystal is a Chinese puzzle box. Chewie scans it and says it is empty. Luke says this is an ancient Sith artifact, known as a Schrödinger box. The matter inside is held in a state of encrypted non-existence. It cannot be cut or forced open. Only solving the combination correctly will pull whatever is stored inside back into time and space and give it physical existence.

Lyra and BB-8 step up to it, her father's notes in hand, and she attempts to open the locked box. With a click, it opens: inside is the sacred scroll.

Elated, she goes to pick it up. Luke calls out a warning. Lyra hesitates, pokes at the scroll with a stick. A cage of lightning flickers into existence around the altar, throwing Lyra back.

With a hum of noise, machinery built into pillars and ramps lights up. Chewie is worried: instruments detect radio beacons in the area going off. There is a powerful emitter on top of the Temple. Flint says, "We've tripped an alarm." He recognizes the code as an Imperial code.

But Naps says the signals are also coming from Flint's black runabout.

Luke says, "It appears that your defection was foreseen, Flint. But only the Jedi would see the future in such detail as to anticipate this. Or a Sith. But their dark fire was extinguished with the death of Palpatine... and my father. That was long ago."

Lyra said, "Or there was no defection. This whole thing has been a trap." She accuses Flint of leading the pursuit after them.

Enemy star destroyers, running dark, now turn on their lights, appear in the sky above the skull-shaped mountains, and begin sweeping the area with searchlights. TIE fighters and fighting droids begin dropping from the belly of the great ships. Explosions and blaster bolts rain down.

Outside, the TIE fighters are landing, and stormtroopers in black armor are gathering in force to rush the bridge over the lava to the door. Naps runs off, looking for a way up to the emitter on the roof, telling Flint, Luke and Chewie to hold the door. Flint puts on his helmet, draws his trident and turns it on.

Lyra sees Flint and the memory comes clear of where she has seen him before: She recognizes the damaged helmet. This is the stormtrooper that killed her father and mother, with the same murder weapon in hand. She reaches for her lightsaber...

(Personally, I thought the idea that she would recognize him from the burn mark on his damaged helmet was ridiculous. In all the years since her parent's death, the trooper has never had his gear cleaned? He never had a parade inspection? He never had the scratches and scars buffed out? C'mon.)

Luke cries out in alarm. Out from the hooded statues of the temple now step nine red glowing ghosts. Count Dooku (aka Darth Tyrannus) is leading them, played by a CGI version of Christopher Lee. The other eight are red ghost versions of Darth Maul and his seven brothers, all with ghastly devil faces like his.

Luke draws his lightsaber; an invisible force swats it from his hand. He clutches his throat, strangling. Invisible power draws him up into the air, legs kicking, and dangles him over the central pit.

Chewie, seeing this from the door, fires a bolt from his bowcaster. It passes through the immaterial spirit being of the dead Dooku and blasts a hole in the wall behind. This red-lit phantom waves a hand at the door controls. The panel slams shut, trapping the raging Chewbacca outside with the oncoming stormtroopers.

In a reprise of the finale of *Return of the Jedi*, Darth Dooku tells Lyra the terrible truth. Her father was not a Jedi, but a Sith. Lyra herself is a Sith, and has been trained wrongly by enemies who fear her power. The sacred scroll she seeks is not a Jedi scroll, and has never been in their lore. It is sacred to the Sith.

For many years it was locked here–her father changed the combination and prevented them from opening the Schrödinger box–and she was kept alive, guided here. Her hands are needed to pick up the scroll for them.

He tells her to unleash her hatred and to strike down the man who killed her parents.

Dooku tells Flint that the Jedi never meant to accept him. His crimes will never be forgiven. Flint looks unsure. Darth Dooku makes a gesture, and Flint's bifork jumps in his hand, and strikes at Lyra. Red sparks fly from her eyes. She and Flint battle.

Meanwhile, Naps, having found a ramp leading to the roof, runs into a squad of Stormtroopers descending from TIE fighters coming down the ramp. He draws a blaster in either hand, and enters a running gun battle.

Down below, the strangling Luke opens his eyes, revealing a terrible look of calmness and power. His eyes light up with an eerie blue light. Blue light issues from his hand and strikes Dooku who screams and vanishes. The remaining eight ghosts shoot Luke with red lightning. He screams horribly.

Meanwhile, Chewbacca, fights like Horatio on the bridge, bloody and magnificent as he is outnumbered, roaring and tossing Stormtroopers left and right like ninepins into the lava, which starts to erupt.

Flint sees Luke suffering, and throws down his weapon, calmly waiting to see whether the Lyra the Sith will strike him dead.

She hesitates. She meditates, turning the red lightning crackling about her blue.

Just then, the blue and ghostly image of Luminara appears. She tells Lyra that forgiveness is the cure to hate, and peace is answer to anger.

The two of them turn and strike the central crystal with the blue aura. The red crystal turns blue, and begins to rise into the air. The red phantoms flinch, blocking the calm blue light with their ghostly fingers as if the calm light hurts them.

Luke recovers. Luminara and Luke now concentrate, commanding the red phantoms to depart. They retreat into the walls.

One of the retreating Sith, who is still robed and hooded never showing his face, offers a polite farewell to Lyra, predicting that she will embrace her heritage, and return to the Dark Side. There has been some internet debate on this point: I think the voice was clearly that of Palpatine. Who else?

Luke rises into the air, following the giant blue lightsaber crystal. It smashes upward into and through the roof of the temple, scattering the stormtroopers surrounding Naps. Naps makes it to the huge dish emitter, and plugs in an instrument from his finger ring, and sends out a message to the Republican Fleet.

Flint and Lyra, together, (after pausing a suspicious moment, and then exchanging a confident look of mutual understanding) haul open the jammed main door, just in time to see Chewbacca, oversized field gun looted from a dead stormtrooper in one hand and bowcaster in the other, cutting the main supports of the bridge, sending the attacking force tumbling to their fiery deaths. Burnt patches mar his fur, and smoke is coming from his wounds. He turns, shows his teeth, gives one last happy grunt of noise, and faints.

The Imperial Star Destroyers now descend toward the Sith Temple. Luke directs a beam of energy from the giant crystal to sever the nearest ship in half. The return fire shatters the crystal. Luke is knocked from his feet, dazed.

Star Destroyers surround the Sith Temple. Gun turrets aim at the outnumbered group. Defeat is inescapable!

But, just at that moment, the Imperial star destroyers are struck from above and start blowing up. Republican battleships by the hundreds emerge from hyperspace, guns blazing.

At the helm of one, we see Admiral Ackbar, exulting that the Imperials have been neatly caught in an ambush. "It's a trap!" He shouts.

A superstar destroyer-sized vessel, with General Solo at the helm, comes diving out of the direction of the dead sun. He utters a war whoop. "Kid! How come I am always saving you? You never watch your back!"

The Imperial Admiral calls a retreat; the Republic blows the retreating fleet to smithereens.

Admiral Thrawn gets away as the boy Emperor raises his little hand, and his ship fades from view in a mysterious red glow.

Aboard the Republican flagship, General Han Solo has apparently come out of retirement. Medals are handed out.

Luminara, in the flesh, is aboard the ship. Lyra is astonished and overjoyed. But how is she not dead? The planet froze! Luminara explains the spores overcame her, and she fainted. We see the scene in flashback: Ood, the tree, was burned only on the surface: his extensive root system is where the real scrolls and records were kept, and he drew her down beneath there. The burning upper stories of the buildings kept the two of them warm until help arrived. Ood sacrificed himself, burning more and more of his substance, to keep her warm as the interstellar cold closed in.

She sent her soul to Nastrond to aid Luke, but not because her body was dead.

Luminara announces that Lyra has achieved the quest. Luke Skywalker is found. A look of mutual understanding, perhaps of sorrow, passes between Luke and Luminara. Maybe a spark of something more.

Luke dubs Lyra to be an official Jedi knight, and graduates her.

She goes to Naps, and asks him how he happened to have a space fleet standing by in a place where the Republic was maintaining a cordon. Napoleon Solo grins and shrugs and says he is actually an officer in the Naval Intelligence Service: a spy.

He actually had permission to enter the Black Sun Nebula to aid her search for the sacred scroll, but since he did not know how far he could trust a turncoat stormtrooper, and the daughter of a Sith, so he could not afford to make it look as if the Republican government was actually looking into the threat.

He hints that there are people among the government who cannot be trusted, and he could not tell anyone his mission, except for the Chairman of the Senate Intelligence Committee.

Also, Napoleon says he has friends in high places. Han Solo, his father, appears, groaning and saying that one day his son will be the death of him! How dare you make me worry? And yells at him for ducking out on his job.

Lyra asks, "His job as a janitor? Or his job as a spy?"

Han Solo guffaws. "Is that what he told you? He is a Senator. He is supposed to be in the Senate, helping guide the Republic through our current crises. I told him his job was to clean up all the mess the previous administration left behind."

Naps says, "I also happen to be the Chairman of the Intelligence Committee. So I have the discretion to hire whoever I would like as an intelligence asset. And, come to think of it, I can also hire someone to serve on the housekeeping staff, just in case Naval Intelligence needed a man able to act as a janitor and sniff around."

Han Solo mocks him gently for having failed his mission: the sacred scroll was just a trap. And the scroll, even if it were real, was gone, leaving them with no hint as to how the Sith find the impossible power to destroy whole solar systems.

BB-8 whistles at him, nudges up to Lyra, and opens up a compartment in its ball shaped body. Out pops the scroll. The robot with his mechanical claw had had no problem reaching through the electrical trap field protecting the scroll while everyone else was busy.

This, Lyra announces, contains the secrets of the construction of how Sith Dark Lords, thousands of generations ago, constructed the mythical artifact known as the Great Eye of Darkness. "It will tell us how to destroy it, I hope. But we have no hope of finding it."

Flint Ansteel enters the cabin, and announces his resolve

to swear fealty to the New Republic. He has been taught all his life that peace and freedom were opposites: that to have one meant to lose the other. He sees now that this was a lie. He had been taught that a Sith cannot become a Jedi; nor a Jedi turn Sith. He now believes each man controls his own destiny.

Lyra still looks skeptical. "But how can we trust you?"

Flint smiles for the first and only time in the film. "Because I know where the Great Eye is hidden. I can lead you there."

Luke reveals that this was why he chose Flint to follow and enlighten.

The film ends on a dark note: the Empire still exists, at least as a fragment, a ghost of its former self, and the power that was behind the Empire, the Sith, even from beyond the grave, still exists and is growing. The Phantom Empire was destroying suns quietly, without claiming credit, and perhaps was using the power sparingly, slowly. Now the masks are torn. The peace is over.

Naps grimly announces that he will introduce a declaration of war into the next meeting of the Senate. The twenty years of peace was just a vacation, not an end.

Cut to a final scene: We see Admiral Thrawn vowing revenge. In an awesome curtain shot, we see the entire hollow planet of Kaas being towed away by a trio of Death Stars, deeper into the Black Sun Nebula.

And roll credits.

The only thing that this movie did not have was "TO BE CONTINUED" in the last frame. But it really captured the look and feel, not only of the first *Star Wars* movie, but, more to the point, it reached back into the old Buck Rogers and Flash Gordon serials, and captured their energy, look, feel, and flavor.

This was pure unabashed fun, folks. I am sure that, somewhere, in some other galaxy far, far away, or some time long ago or in times to come, a world curiously like our Earth exists, a nearly perfect twin. But it will have this one difference: their Star Wars franchise fell into the hands of incompetent boobs who cared more about political correctness than telling a story.

I pity the audiences on that world. The will never know what they might have had.

I will review the next movie in the trilogy *The Last Dark Lord*, when time permits.

5

FOOLED BY HEINLEIN FOR FORTY YEARS

Here is my sad tale of my deception at the hands of the Dean of Science Fiction, Robert Heinlein, which I pass along only to show that one's most cherished beliefs can sometimes be revised by experience:

There is a scene in Robert Heinlein's *Glory Road*, where the hero, Oscar Gordon, is traveling among barbarians from some outer dimension. Their custom is to share their daughters' love (or wives') with traveling heroes for a night or two, in hopes of fathering good stock. Oscar the hero unwittingly offends the custom by refusing the copulate with the daughter of the local lord, his host. For this he is tongue-lashed by the heroine for being provincial, backward, rude, and stupid; at some personal risk to himself, he returns to the mansion of the barbarian lord, apologizes manfully, commits orgy, fornicates with gusto, and goes on his way with the heroine on his arm, her eyes shining with admiration. This heroine is named Star; the names of the nice young ladies with whom he ruts are nowhere mentioned.

Even as a youth, I prided myself (and my pride was immoderate when I was young, I am afraid, and may not be moderate now) on being a careful and skeptical thinker. But it was not until I was 41, some three decades after first reading that scene, that I thought, for the first time, there was something wrong with the picture Mr. Heinlein paints.

What if Oscar the hero had fathered a child during his one-night stand? Does a father have no moral obligations running to a child, to love, to cherish, to protect, to see to its upbringing? The mother of Moses sent her babe off in a basket down the river because the soldiers of Pharaoh were coming to kill it; but Oscar here apparently is sending his child down the river because he wishes to enjoy a momentary sexual pleasure with an unnamed woman, and because he does not wish to offend the ugly customs of outlandish people.

I look at the perfect face of my own cherubic child, and I wonder, what kind of man would let his child be raised as a bastard by strangers? If the child is a daughter, will she be sent to whore around with other wandering heroes?

If the customs of the land had demanded our hero sacrifice a captive to Tezcatlipoca, would his bitchy girlfriend have brow-beaten him into doing that, too?

The bitchy girlfriend turns out to be an Empress, and she marries the hero. I must laugh. What kind of girl would marry a man (or even give him the time of day) after he has sported with harlots? How did Clytemnestra react when her husband lord Agamemnon came back from the wars, having slept with many a golden slave-girl from Illium? She killed him with an axe in the bath. Compare Heinlein with Aeschylus. Who do you think knows more about how women really act?

For that matter, compare Heinlein with Robert E. Howard. Solomon Kane, puritan adventurer from New England, travels the world slaying troglodytes, vampires and witch-queens descended from the survivors of devil-worshipping Atlanteans. He would not take off his hat for a king of Europe or Asia, or bow to an alien idol, even if he might die for his unbending defiance. Who is more the hero?

In a word, I was snookered. Skeptic that I thought I was, it did not occur to me to question the amoral, epicurean and hedonistic philosophy put across by Mr. Heinlein in his books. It seemed so much common sense. I had never stopped to wonder: would Socrates, or Cato of Utica (or Sir Galahad or Kimball Kinnison of the Galactic Patrol, or Frodo Baggins of Bag End) have done what Oscar Gordon did?

I was too young to know, and too arrogant to believe, that hedonism leads to nihilism. It is a dead-end philosophy: a hedonist has no reason to praise temperance; an epicurean has no reason to praise courage; the live-for-today libertine has no use for prudence; man who, like Oscar Gordon, says that all customs are merely arbitrary cultural constructions, and refuses to see the difference between cruelty and civilization, such a man has no sense of justice.

I assure you I was as settled in my beliefs as man can be: I had studied the premises and principles with great skepticism and subjected the whole structure of philosophy to pitiless logic, and tested and retested every link in my chain of reasoning. But I was inexperienced. Non-Euclidean geometry is also perfectly logical, but only experience can tell you whether or not Euclid's fifth postulate describes the world we see, or not.

'Cultural relativism' or 'when in Rome, do as the Romans' is not taken seriously by Heinlein, or anyone else, except in minor manners like courtesy (take off your shoes in a mosque, for example). If it were taken seriously, Heinlein would have written a scene where Oscar Gordon is passing through the Friendly Planet Harmony, run by strict Puritans, and when he tried to kiss a girl, Star would upbraid him and send him back to Cotton Mather and Lord

Cromwell for a ducking, which Oscar would endure like a man.

Oscar would then become dispassionate and emotionless on planet Vulcan and adopt a touchy sense of honor when on planet Klingon, become a duty-bound stoic on planet Romulus, and would sniff spice up his nose and obey the rules of the rigid class system (Faufreluches) when on planet Dune. He would then practice sodomy when on planet O, for such is the custom there, and admit himself to be a sexual pervert when on planet Gethen, for so he would be there, and practice cannibalism when on planet Tschai, or planet Geta, or even on Mars, for such is the custom in these places. And when in Rome, he would bow to the Pope and kiss his ring, for such is the custom inRome.

Somehow, I cannot imagine Oscar Gordon doing any of these things.

The fact of the matter is, one cannot be both a cultural relativist and a revolutionary. The revolutionary proposes changing the culture. A cultural relativist can never propose such a change. What standard could be used? A cultural relativist, were he honest, would hold his own culture to the same standards as a foreign culture, and say that our laws, traditions, and customs cannot be changed or criticized—for if the only yardstick of what is considered right or wrong comes from the culture, well, obviously this applies to Christendom (aka Western Culture) as well.

One particular unrealistic aspect of the scene in *Glory Road* is that Star the Sexy Space Babe did not warn or coach Oscar beforehand that he was expected to stud-service the whores and father bastards to be abandoned. Instead, the author makes it clear that having any reservations about performing the mating act with a female with whom one has no intent to mate is so wrongheaded as to need no comment: why *of course* Oscar should have known without being told that the rules of biology and romance and ethics were ass-backwards on this planet! It's utterly obvious!

And if the host sends up a pre-adolescent girl, younger than Mohamed's child bride, why, you are supposed to commit statutory rape at once, rather than offend the iron-clad law of hospitality! And if the host himself had come by at midnight and expected homo-sex, good manners would have demanded you grip your ankles and present your plump buttocks immediately, with no explanations needed beforehand! And you must honor the corpse of the ancestral grandmother by fornicating with the sacred mummy! And then service the sacred totem animal, which, for our clan, is the ewe. And wipe your feet on the mat before entering someone's house! Didn't your mother teach you anything?!— or does the rule about "Doing the Romans when in Rome" only apply to sexual deviations that we personally like?

6

SCIENCE FICTION AND WONDER
AND HUMBUG

DOES *Left Behind* count as SciFi? Do things that are heavily influenced by religion like Dune, Star Wars, Battlestar Galactica, and others count as being religious in nature?

Excellent question! Allow me to wax pedantic:

Let me start by saying I am not qualified to answer. I have not read the *Left Behind* series. My opinion is necessarily based on hearsay and ignorance. But I used to work for a newspaper, so ignorance of the topic is no excuse for not filling up the column space!

At a guess, from what I hear of it, I would not consider *Left Behind* to fit my definition of science fiction.

On firmer ground, I can say I do not consider the science fiction stories *Dune* or *Battlestar Galactica*, nor the space-opera fairy story *Star Wars* to be religious fiction.

Science fiction stories are poetical or emotional accounts of man's relationship to the scientific view of the natural universe and the Darwinian view of the origins of life. They are basically wonder stories about the wonders (or horrors) of science, of change and progress. Fantasy stories are the nostalgia of the scientific age for the magic of the medieval and pagan world view, or, at least, the view reflected in their epics, chansons, folk tales, and wonder stories. Religious stories are those primarily meant for edifying the faith, whether they contain elements of wonder or not.

Science fiction by this definition is the opposite of, for example, the Aeneid of Virgil, which showed the eternal laws of the divine gods and the eternal order of the universe as establishing the eternal city of Rome and her central place in it. Science fiction is about change and emphasizes the instability, the non-eternal nature, of those things we would otherwise take for granted, whether the change is, for example, the degeneration of Man into Eloi and Morlock by AD 802701, or the change is the rise of Big Brother in Airstrip One by AD 1984.

All stories, to some degree, are a humbug.

They are make-believe, a humbug willingly believed by the audience for the duration of the story. So all stories, even the most fantastical, must contain an element that makes the audience willing (for the duration) to believe it, to grant the hypothetical, so to speak, to step into the dream.

In a science fiction story the humbug is scientific, or based (however loosely) on the scientific world view. When the Time Traveler of H.G. Wells sees the fate of man, the humbug is a machine that travels through the dimension of time, and so the story is a scientific romance; but when Scrooge sees his fate, he is escorted there by a ghost in a dream or vision, so the humbug there is ghost-story stuff, fantasy.

Much ink has been spilled on the question of whether unscientific humbug can be legitimately used in science fiction? Does the science have to be real? I dismiss such questions with a supercilious wave of my snuffbox. Science fiction has never been about real science; it has always been about believable make-believe science. What makes the

humbug believable is not how realistic the science is—
although that helps, particularly in the sub-genre called hard
SF—no, what makes the humbug believable is the willingness
of the audience is to believe it. The primary thing that makes
the audience willing is if the humbug either intellectually or
emotionally fits with (and flatters) their world view, which,
for the science fiction reading public, is the scientific world
view.

If the humbug intellectually fits, it is Jules Verne-type
fiction, or hard SF; if it emotionally fits, it is H.G. Wells-type
fiction, or soft SF.

The difference between hard and soft SF is the difference
between being shot to the moon in a shell that obeys the real
laws of real ballistics, or floating to the moon in a sphere
made of anti-gravity alloy; it is the difference between riding
the submersible ironclad Nautilus through the sea or riding
the Time Machine through the aeons.

So even a story which takes place in an openly Christian
world-view, such as the planetary trilogy by CS Lewis,
provided it has even a veneer of elements from the scientific
world view, as the space-ship of Weston in *Out of the Silent
Planet*, it becomes science fiction by the definition I am
proposing; but where those scientific elements are missing,
as in *That Hideous Strength*, it either becomes a fantasy (if the
supernatural elements are meant to be regarded as unreal) or
simply a mainstream fiction (if the supernatural elements are
meant to be regarded as real).

By "meant to be regarded" I do not mean the stance of the
man writing the book; I mean the stance of the book itself.
CS Lewis, I doubt not, believed that 'Maleldil' was real, since
this is merely another name for God; but I doubt he believed
Merlin the Magician would rise from the grave in England's
hour of greatest need. That is on the one hand. On the other,
Maleldil and Merlin are treated both as story elements with

an equal degree of make-believe in *That Hideous Strength*. The believability of Lewis's "fairy-tale for grownups" depends on how believable Merlin appears when he appears. (And I, for one, regard Lewis' as the most believable portrayal of that mythic figure I have encountered in any book.)

That may be a confusing way of putting it. Let me try again:

A man who believes in ghosts reading a story by a writer who believes in ghosts, *and* the story is meant by the author and taken by the reader to be a fictional but realistic account of something which, no matter how unlikely or romanticized, they both regard as legitimately part of the real world is no more science fiction or fantasy than an unlikely or romanticized pirate story would be when told by and told to an author and audience who believed pirates are real.

But a ghost-story, even when told by and to people who believe in ghosts, which introduces an element of the scientific world view to provide verisimilitude, or which introduces a speculation or extrapolation, no matter how farfetched, which is part of the scientific world view (such as relativity), or part of the romance surrounding the scientific world view (such as time travel) then it is a science fiction story.

By this definition, Shakespeare's *Hamlet* is not in the fantasy story genre, and the genre does not change whether or not the audience believes in ghosts. In the television show *Veronica Mars* the teen detective sees her dead friend in a dream, but this show would not suddenly become a fantasy story if the ghost were real. On the other hand, *The Ghost and Mrs. Muir* is a fantasy story, because the ghost is akin to the Witch in *Bewitched* and the Genii in *I Dream of Jeannie* and the Martian in *My Favorite Martian*—the whole point of the show is the introduction into ordinary life of a fantastic element that has no natural explanation.

If your ghosts create electromagnetic disturbances when they walk, and can be captured by beams shot from unlicensed nuclear accelerators into magnetic containment units, as in *Ghostbusters*, at that point, ghosts or no ghosts, it is a science fiction story, because you are using elements from the scientific world view to perform your exorcisms.

By this definition, *A Wrinkle in Time* is science fiction and not fantasy even though it has witches and angels and demons in it, because the witches are depicted as space aliens, and the angels and demons, while clearly supernatural, are inhibitors of other planets and parallel dimensions. You could not read *Wrinkle in Time* to Dante without stopping to explain the Kepler model of the solar system and the Einstein model of the spacetime continuum. The fantasy elements exist within the naturalistic model of the modern scientific world view.

Likewise, a Gnostic fairy tale like *Childhood's End* is still science fiction, even though it has cartoony devil-creatures with batwings and horns, and ends with the enlightened spirits rising to the Pleroma and achieving unity with Godhead—but the humbug is scientific humbug and not magical humbug, and the Overlords and their Cosmic Over-Mind they serve as described as created by evolution, that is, as natural beings not as supernatural, and so the tale is science fiction.

In other words, the story is science fiction if the audience must first understand the basic scientific model of the universe. I mean only the most basic idea: it is Science Fiction when the wandering stars are globes like Terra containing mortal beings, not spiritual realms as in Dante. When Cavor or Barbican travel to the moon, they do not meet the soul of Piccarda Donati, the Empress Constance, or other blessed spirits who broke their vows in life.

While a purist might insist that a movie where spaceships,

engines roaring, make banked turns like World War One fighter jets, and make the Kessel run in less than twelve parsecs is as far outside the scientific model of the universe as the Ptolemaic spheres of Dante, I would allow space opera to be science fiction because it is in the spirit of the scientific age, and captures the romance of science, even if scientifically illiterate. Call me an "impurist" if you will.

But, by Grabthar's Hammer and Klono's carbotanium claws, before you exile *Star Wars* and its mystical "Force" to the fantasy wilderness outside the genre of science fiction, tell me how humbugs like the Mind Meld of Mr. Spock, the transporter beams and warps drives of *Star Trek*, the mind-controlling Slaver race, teleportation, stasis-fields, ringworld material and breeding for luck from *Ringworld*, the history-controlling Seldon Plan and mind-controlling Psychohistorians of *Foundation*, the Espers from *Starship Troopers*, the angels (complete with halo and wings!) from *Stranger in a Strange Land*, or the magical monkey-evolving Monolith spacewarpy magic door ("My God, it's full of stars") from *2001: A Space Odyssey* fit in to the standard scientific model of the cosmos, or any model.

Let us turn to the next question—what makes a story religious?

Myself, I do not regard merely having a character or a society portrayed as having or obeying a religious creed as significant. The religion of the Fremen of Dune, which is descends from Zen Buddhism and Sunni teachings, does not bring the story out of the definition of science fiction, nor more than does the Orange-Catholic religion of the thinly disguised outer space version of the Byzantine Empire of Shaddam IV and the Bene Gesserit sisterhood. I do not see this as different in principle from a story where John Carter, Warlord of Mars, runs across the odd and sinister cult of the Therns of Barsoom, or Conan facing the giant snake worshiped as a god by the Serpent-Cult of the sinister serpent-men of Valusia.

Outer space people worship space gods. This has been true in the very earliest strata of science fiction history. In *Skylark of Space* (1928), the green-skinned natives of Kondal (a favorite skin color for space people ever since) make a reference to "the First Cause" as a euphemism for their monotheistic god (to my mind, a repellant and Darwinian god).

Again, in *Starmaker* by Olaf Stapledon (1937) a monotheistic god is not only the McGuffin driving the plot, but comes on stage as a character in the apocalyptic climax at the end of this universe in a vision of multiple universes (once again, a repellant and Darwinian monotheistic god).

Before we Christians complain that our god is under-represented in the science fiction genre, I ask them to name for me the pirate stories, wild west stories, detective stories or even (oddly enough) ghost stories and vampire stories where there is any mention of a god at all, or hint of divine presence, much less a Christian one. If anything, science fiction contains more mention and more speculation about gods and godlike things than other genres.

Science fiction certainly comments about the role of religion in society—usually societies where savage green men are about to sacrifice a gorgeous yet nubile half-clad space princess to an insane all-powerful computer they worship as an idol, so the commentary is usually quite sophomoric; but then again, our beloved genre contains magical monkey-evolving Monoliths and Seldon Plans and Ringworld material and faster-than-light drives, so no one expects our theology or anthropology to be more sophisticated than our physics.

The story of *Dune* is certainly about religion: Paul Muad-Dib is certainly a messiah-figure, but there is no implication that a character in the story named God actually selected Paul to lead the Fremen jihad—rather, the clear implication is that genetics and mind-training and alien chemicals gave Paul Way Cool mind powers, but these powers are something that exist as scientific non-supernatural phenomena in that background. The Bene Gesserit Witches are not really witches, not in the sense that Hermione Grangier or Samantha Stephens or Glinda the Good is a Witch.

So I would not call *Dune* a "religious" story for the simple fact that it is not read for the edification of the faith, or of any faith. It is not like *Pilgrim's Progress*, whose main point is edification of the faith.

Star Wars is less religious than a sober work contemplating religious themes, such as *The Spectre* from DC comics or that insightful meditation on the intricacies of Taoism known as *Big Trouble in Little China*. I have written an entire essay on the question of religion in *Star Wars*,and which I will not repeat here. Curious readers can purchase *Star War on Trial* (November, 2015) edited by David Brin and Matthew Stover, for a detailed investigation of the question.

Here I will say only that 'The Force' in *Star Wars* is, by design, the most vague and undemanding of mystical humbugs, and the point is to allow space-samurai with laser swords to do backflips, catch blaster bolts, and throw objects with their minds, or shoot lightning from their fingertips.

Battlestar Galactica is a slightly different question, because it is modeled on some events from the Book of Mormon, and because, at least in the original series, supernatural good and bad angels came on stage as characters. In that respect, it is like, for example, Orson Scott Card's *Homegoing* series, which had similar themes.

I assume a Mormon could achieve some religious edification from the work, the same way I receive religious edification from, for example, *The Silver Chair* by CS Lewis: but in each case, I don't think that is the primary purpose of the work.

Contrast this with *The Screwtape Letters*, where I think religious instruction is the primary purpose of the work—it is not a horror story nor a ghost story, but a thinly disguised series of lectures on matters particular to the Christian faith.

In this way, the religious stories are like love stories or horror stories. A horror story with a scientific element in the background, such as *Frankenstein*, is still shelved with other horror stories because its primary purpose is to arouse a certain emotion in the mind of the reader.

Does having Way Cool mind powers make the story a fantasy? Is it a fantasy if a Luke Skywalker is able to perform psychokinesis, or Mr. Spock able to perform a Mind Meld, or the Gray Lensman Kimball Kinneson able to see through walls, or Jommy Cross able to read minds, or Gilbert Gosseyn able to teleport, or Michael Valentine Smith able to do all of the above?

I would say it depends on the humbug used to explain why and how these people have these powers. If the powers are granted by divine Providence or a Deal with the Devil, it is different than if they are granted by Mentor of Arisia or the Old Ones of Mars.

You can have a story about the rise of the Anti-Christ without it being science fiction—*Rosemary's Baby*, for example, I would shelve next to *Dracula* and *The Shining* in the horror section rather than next to *Galactic Patrol* and *Starship Troopers*.

I do not mean to make my nice, simple definition "science fiction is the mythology of the scientific era" any more complex than it seems, but I have to add one thing: merely writing in a background of a religion some people believe and others do not does not put the book into or out of the science fiction or fantasy genre. I am a Christian: I believe the events of the Apocalypse will take place either literally or symbolically, as described, and I believe echoes or types of those events have already happened.

But if I wrote or read a fictional account of these events, whether or not I defined the tale as fantasy would depend on the type of humbug used to make the make-believe seem believable.

If the anti-Christ came from Mars, as he does in Robert Heinlein's *Stranger in a Strange Land*, it is science fiction. (Oh, come on: I know Mr. Heinlein did not *mean* his satire to be read in that way, but as a textbook example of a false messiah, you might admit Mike the Martian preaching eugenics and Free Love fits the bill.)

If the anti-Christ is a talking Ape from Talking-Animal-Land, who preaches that Aslan is the same as Tash, it is fantasy.

If the story took place in the modern world in the day after tomorrow, and the wove real events in the Middle East into the plot, it would be a mainstream fiction or political thriller, and I would not automatically shelve the book with *Galactic Patrol* merely because one of the characters was a modern-day Nero or Anti-Christ, even if he has Way Cool Mind Powers.

Let me put this last point another way: as far as pirate stories go, *Treasure Island* is a pirate story, and so is *Pirates of the Caribbean*, and merely having ghosts in the pirate story does not make it not a pirate story. On the other hand, there are pirates both in *Galactic Patrol* and in *On Stranger Tides*, which I would call science fiction and fantasy respectively, because the humbug used to explain the make-believe are either scientific (as the Lens of Arisia granting Way Cool Mind Powers) or fantasy explanations (as the lack of iron in the New World allowing ancient magics to thrive there which died off in Europe).

A story in a Christian background, such as *A Christmas Carol* or *Angel On My Shoulder* or *Heaven Can Wait*, even if written by a writer and read by a reader who does not take that background as true, is still a mainstream and not an SFF story for the same reason a pirate story with a ghost in it is a pirate story and not a ghost story even for readers who don't believe in ghosts.

As I said, I have not read the *Left Behind* books. I don't know if the book's primary purpose is the edification of the faith or if the writer is merely writing a thriller taking the events in the Apocalypse and playing them out in the modern day. If the book is a thriller set in the modern day, I would say it is not science fiction.

The religious beliefs of the reader and writer, as far as my definition is concerned, do not matter. It is the way the elements are handled inside the book that matter.

So the reader who does not believe in the Christian faith should not shelve *Left Behind* with *The Wizard Of Oz* in the fantasy section merely on the basis of that disbelief, any more than my pagan friends should shelve *The Lightning Thief* or *The Dresden Files* next to *Gone With The Wind* or *Hunt For Red October* in the mainstream fiction section on the basis of their belief in Zeus or White Magic.

7

WRITING WITH AN AX TO GRIND

WHEN IS A STORY NOT A STORY? At what point does it become propaganda?

Propaganda is that which is designed to manipulate readers into an ideology. Stories are different in an essential way, for they differ in kind, not just in degree.

The topic is a difficult one because it does not lend itself to simple answers. We must proceed carefully, like explorers in a mire, since too bold a step, much less leaping to any conclusions, might suck the conversation into the swamp of mutual incomprehension.

Let us also distinguish several cases:

(1) a story which gives honest, non-strawmanlike, portrayal of both sides of a question is not propaganda. This is a difference of kind.

(2) the more logic and less sophistry is I involved makes the propaganda more tolerable. This is a difference of degree.

(3) a story that persuades the reader on a point that is not related to an ideology is not propaganda. This rule is difficult

to apply, because modern ideologies attempt to be as all-embracing as religion, so that opinions about women or the weather become political statements. This could be a difference of kind when the story is not related to an ideology; or a difference in degree if the relationship is tentative or indirect.

(4) A story where the message is skillfully woven into the tale may or may not be propaganda depending on its intent and point, but how obvious and obnoxious the message-preaching becomes is a difference of degree.

(5) All stories portray an author's assumed worldview. Not all world views are primarily political. Not all stories aim at persuading the reader to adopt the author's worldview for longer than the duration of the story.

(6) All stories have a moral that can be read into it. Not all stories are written to moralize.

In this essay, let us see if we can explore these six points, and perhaps we can be excused if this is a rambling exploration filled with digressions. The subject matter is mazelike; we may need to turn and return at several points.

Let us therefore, with due caution, use the definition given above for propaganda. This definition refers to the purpose or 'final cause' for which the story is meant: namely, to manipulate readers into an ideology.

This definition does not explicitly say that it is the intention in the writer's mind, as opposed to the reader's mind or even the muse's. The definition tacitly assumes that stories have an innate final cause independent of the conscious intention of the writer. The definition also tacitly assumes that the innate final cause of any given story, at least in theory, can be discovered by an onlooker. Neither of these assumptions, at the moment, has been given any support. For the moment, let us accept for the sake of argument that they are so: a more rigorous proof is a question for another day.

Yet another unspoken assumption behind the definition is that propaganda is one-sided. Some writers have an ax to grind.

A propagandist, like an attorney loyal only to his client, will argue his client's case, and does not bring up any points helpful to the opposition. An artist, if he is honestly presenting an image of the world as it is or as it should be, will give both sides of the argument, because in nature there are two sides to each question, if not more. An artist may be indeed quite loyal to his burning vision of the world, but an attorney is a partisan loyal to a cause, not to a vision.

The attorney is trying to get a result, that is, to persuade a jury; whereas the poet is trying capture in a web of words a reality somehow more real than reality itself, as strange as Norse gods catching Fenrir in a gossamer strand made of nine impossible things.

A propagandist is even less honest: he does not actually argue the case nor even tell the jurors that there are two sides to the case. He uses rhetoric rather than logic, uses appeals to emotion and uses other fundamentally indirect and dishonest tactics. The perfect propagandist changes his victim's mind without the victim even being aware of the operation.

Contrariwise, philosophy confronts a judge with two opposite view points and calls on him to use his dispassionate reasoning to render a verdict. Propaganda is the mere opposite of this. Propaganda lulls rather than awakens the judgment.

The definition confines itself to 'ideologies'—a term we have not defined. Again, this is another unspoken assumption. This would seem to imply that there is some real difference between an ideology versus, say, a philosophy, a religion, a worldview, a vision, a belief, or merely an opinion.

For the purpose of this argument, an 'ideology' is defined

as a system of abstract ideas integral to a model of ideal (or at least improved) human life that either explains or dismisses all of life's basic questions, but only where the model emphasizes social, political, economic, or ethical abstractions. By this definition, Libertarianism would be an ideology, but Ricardo's Theory of Comparative advantage would not. Communism would be an ideology but Christianity would not. Existentialism would be an ideology, but generic exhortations to courage would not.

A good rule of thumb is that any word ending in an -ism refers to an ideology. Conservatives sometimes claim their worldview is not an ideology because it restricts itself to concrete and pragmatic approaches to political and ethical questions: be that as it may, by this definition, Conservatism is an ideology.

So, let us now face the question, first arming ourselves with examples.

I can think of three science fiction books off the top of my head which clearly fall into the propaganda category and are propaganda throughout: *Starship Troopers* by Heinlein, which promoted civic militarism; *Atlas Shrugged* by Ayn Rand which promoted a philosophical variant of Libertarianism called (at least by its founder) Objectivism; *The Amber Spyglass* by Philip Pullman which promoted a particularly vile variant of death-obsessed anticlerical atheism.

(If some maven of the Linnean society wants to argue that *Atlas Shrugged* is not science fiction, I will defer that for another day. For our purposes, anything in the same genre as *Nineteen Eighty-Four* or *Brave New World* is science fiction).

The question is whether all other stories differ in kind or merely in degree from these nakedly propagandist efforts. A thing differs in degree if it is the same in essence, differing only in quantity, a long river as opposed to a short river;

whereas a difference in kind means it is of a different species, a river of blood as opposed to a river of water. The added confusion is that there are cases where the differences in degree are so great that it becomes a difference in kind. A river that is so short that it only flows a few feet would not be a river. A river that is dry in summer is still a river; a river dry year round is a canyon.

I must add a word of caveat. In the first two cases (Heinlein and Rand) the propaganda was undisguised and consequently so honest that we could, if we wished, call these philosophical or rhetorical novels rather than propaganda novels.

No propaganda was being sneaked in past the unwary eyes of the reader: it was propaganda, but it was not sneaky at all! A speech from a school instructor or radio program would periodically interrupt the plot to use rhetoric and argument to promote an ideology. It was a subtle as a blow on the bridge of the nose by a ball peen hammer.

Philip Pullman's work, by contrast, differs in degree (it is less skillful and also less honest) but not in kind. It is likewise propaganda, but not open enough merely to have speeches by sockpuppets uttering the author's opinions. It was also as subtle as a ball peen hammer, but in this case, that was not by design, but by the clumsiness of Pullman.

Pullman also gave no arguments, that is, no reasoned discourse. He merely used emotional examples and rhetoric. He does not, for example, utter the Problem of Pain or dwell on the epistemological difficulties of knowing whether an infinite being exists: he just makes God a foolish cripple and Lamech a foolish rapist.

The Chronicles of Narnia, on the other hand, contain so much that is solid storytelling, and worthy of appreciation by non-christians, and its propaganda on behalf of Christianity is so well woven into this storytelling, all this makes it unclear whether Narnia differs in kind as well as in degree from these more obviously propagandist books. It is in the twilight zone.

And, besides, if we cling too literally to the definition I gave, Narnia could not be propaganda by definition, since Christianity is not an ideology. We need another word to refer to stories that try to persuade the reader to adopt a viewpoint or vision or worldview aside from an ideological one, and so I propose the term 'morality tale.'

All of Aesop's fables, by this definition, are morality tales. They propose what, if you examine it closely, can be seen as a rather cynical and hard-headed world view, such as what one might have heard preached by Diogenes or practiced by Alcibiades.

The Pilgrim's Progress by Bunyan is pure morality tale, so much so that it is paramount in the genre of the allegory. Allegories are the peculiar genre where all other elements of storytelling, character, plot, verisimilitude and so on, are thrown aside to make room for unambiguous symbolism. An allegory is pure morality tale undisguised.

The Narnia books form a blatant attempt to teach specific Christian moral principles or elements of Christian faith, and are morality tales, but also contain a great deal of pure storytelling that seems to be storytelling for its own sake, art for art's sake.

By contrast, Lord of the Rings takes place in a Christian moral atmosphere, but is not a morality tale. It may indeed persuade some reader to take Christianity seriously (albeit in my experience Lord of the Rings persuades the readers I know to take Wicca and Neopaganism seriously) but in any case evangelization is not its final cause.

Likewise, *A Wizard Of Earthsea* takes place in a Taoist moral atmosphere and the moral of the story, the moving climax where Sparrowhawk understands and overcomes the nature of the deadly shadow that is his enemy, is so clear a lesson of Taoism that Lao Tzu himself could have used the example of Sparrowhawk as a parable.

There are two dimensions of propaganda to keep in mind. One is the depth of the message being preached, and the other is the frequency.

To measure the depth, use the following rule of thumb: if the message were removed, would the rest of the story still stand? For example, in *Starship Troopers* the answer is clearly a resounding No. It is not a war story. The fighting scenes are few and far between and sketchy to the point of zenlike reductionism. It is a story about the pragmatic morality of fighting, the patriotic duty to fight. Remove the speeches and everything in the tale used to buttress or exemplify the points made in the speeches, and the entire story is gone.

Again, try to imagine *Atlas Shrugged* without the struggle between the productive and arch-rational supermen and the vampiric irrational socialists, and there is no story. I suppose there is sort of a harsh and angular love story between Dagny and Reardon, but since the ultimate resolution of that plotline is forced by the author's peculiar theories of the metaphysical foundations of love and romance, even that would have to be dropped.

Likewise, again, while parts of *The Golden Compass* or *The Subtle Knife* might be preserved without the anticlerical message, there is no story in *Amber Spyglass* aside from the struggle between the good freethinking atheists and the Evil Church of Evil and their clown-like god who evaporates upon exposure to air.

Frequency is another thing. It is common enough in movies and books to hide a Leftwing 'sucker punch' beneath what otherwise seems an innocent story, or whip out an anti-Bush joke in the third act that has nothing to do with the story, or suddenly make an old wizard or a comedy relief Viking a sodomite, in order to make the homosexual disorder seems harmless and unremarkable. These are called sucker punches because they are the opposite of deep propaganda: their whole effect comes from them being unexpected to the point of being extraneous.

So imagine listening to a comedian telling ninety-nine jokes about his mother-in-law, and one remark that is not a joke at all to the effect that everyone who regards homosexual acts as sinful, or even imprudent, is a hateful bigot with no right to a polite hearing: and Christ was evil for preaching sexual purity, and the Antichrist is Our Master.

In this case, the ninety-nine jokes were nothing more than the patter of a confidence trickster, a con job to get you to lower your guard, to lull your suspicions, so he could punch you while you were nodding, you sucker. When you reel from the blow, you dare not voice any objection, lest you be accused of being overly sensitive or hysterical "Why look! You complain about one joke out of Ninety-Nine! Only Batwoman is a Lesbian out of countless comic book heroines! All the other wizards of Hogwarts are heterosexual! You are oddly obsessed with what is a trivial bit of character development!"

The only sucker punch book I can bring to mind is *Time and Again* by Jack Finney. This is what I like to call a mainstream science fiction book, that is, a book that uses a science fiction premise to get the action started, but does not call on the reader to make any science fiction leaps of the imagination. After some two hundred pages of love story and mystery, suddenly the main character decides that, in order to prevent time travelers from changing the past, and making pre-Castro Cuba into a territory of the United States a la Puerto Rico, he erases his boss at the CIA from the timestream via preventing his parents from meeting; in effect, killing him before he is born. Now, the author apparently thought that it was so obvious that Cuba should be communist that, aside from one aside, he does not regard it as necessary to argue the point, or even mention it.

This was a total Leftwing sucker punch, because nothing in the book leading up to that moment (and it happens on page 389!!) gives even the slightest clue that the character or the author was a pro-Communist. He merely treats it as a given, as if he is pretending the folly and evil of the United States is beyond question, beyond discussion, and the goodness of Castro does not need to be mentioned. It is pro-pinko agitprop, pure and simple, and it comes out of left field (so to speak) to blindside any reader.

A book like *Atlas Shrugged* hammers its one point relentlessly in every sentence of every paragraph of every page in an awe-inspiring display of auctorial monomania, or, if you prefer, purity of devotion.

But a Sucker Punching book like *Time and Again* is not the opposite of *Atlas Shrugged*, it is merely surprise blitz rather than trench warfare, concentrated propaganda rather than diffused. The difference is not one of kind nor one of degree but only one of tactic.

Let us make the matter even more complicated by mentioning how well or how poorly the propaganda is woven into the books. While I personally have far less distaste for propaganda skillfully executed, as in the movie *Alexander Nevsky*, the skillfulness might make the story easier to sell, but it would still be propaganda.

Remember, our definition assumes that the final cause of the story can be discovered by an attentive reader, without being concerned with the author's intent, in much the same way as one can tell a wing's purpose is to fly, even the wings of Ostriches and Penguins, without consulting the creator of the wing (Darwin's blind natural selection or some angel with a sense of humor, take your pick).

This means that a skillful story whose structure and meaning makes it clear that the point is to change the mind of the reader and convince him to adopt an ideology, that is a propaganda story—that the story is well done enough to be read and enjoyed by people outside the author's ideological circle is indifferent to this definition. This would be a difference of degree (more intrusive versus less intrusive propaganda) but not of kind.

Let us make the matter more complicated again by looking at other messages which can be carried in a story.

In the Lensman series by E.E. 'Doc' Smith, the author makes a point about slave societies being unable to cooperate; this point is central to the resolution of at least one major plotline and two minor battle scenes. At the time when he wrote, in the 1930s, the idea that centrally controlled fascist or socialist societies were superior to democracies because they were better organized was universally acclaimed among the intelligentsia. This idea clearly was political, as it was in defense of democracy, and it is argued, that is, a reason is given in the mouth of a character to show why this is so, and the author clearly meant it to refer to the real world. It was not an argument about whether gold dragons have hotter fire than black dragons. Does this count as propaganda?

In Isaac Asimov's most famous short story, 'Nightfall', a certain view of humankind, namely that we are plastic and passive receptacles of our upbringing and conditioning, is inherent in the story and is its only point and moral. This grim and dismal view of man is the center of the story, in fact, which is deliberately meant as a rebuke to Emmerson's conceit that if the stars were seen only once a thousand years, men would adore the Creator. Asimov smirks and says, no, men would go mad. Does this count as propaganda?

In *Stranger in a Strange Land* by Heinlein, Jubal Hershaw gives a long speech about sculpture and art that has nothing to do with anything before or after, is not integral to the character, and seems to be the author's opinion that he wanted to talk about, putting his sprawling plot on hold to do so. It is one of Heinlein's typical sockpuppet moments. Does this count as propaganda?

Here we have to make a very narrow distinction which falls across the intent of the story. If the point of the additional message is to manipulate the reader into adherence to an ideology, the answer is yes, it is propaganda; but if the point of the additional message is that it is either (1) a part of the author's world view integral to him (2) a part of the story integral to it or (3) an aside of interest to the author, then, in any of those cases, it is not propaganda.

This is true even if the same point or same idea (as the steadiness of democracy, the plastic nature of man, the edifying nature of art) in another context would be propaganda. If I get into a fistfight to impress a girl, this is different than if I get into a fistfight because I am belligerent and an onlooker who is a girl happens to be impressed. The difference is the purpose of the addition.

To make this clear, let me use a negative example from my own career. In *Count to a Trilion*, I propose a future where the English-speaking nations have collapsed, and India and South America are the centers of economic and military power. Anglo-American values, such as the equality of the classes of man, have been replaced by Hindu values, such as the inequality of the castes of man. The Hindus and Spaniards launch the world's first multi-decade interstellar expedition: the crew is all male. However, upon its return, the expedition has aboard a sixteen-year-old superhuman girl allegedly the dead Captain's daughter. This is something the author intended as a mystery to puzzle the reader and the main character: how could anyone be born during an all-male expedition?

One reviewer barfed scorn and scathing all over my book, on the grounds that it is racist (because I portrayed non-White Asians and South Americans as being in economic ascendency over North American non-Whites, I suppose) and sexist (because I was able to imagine a future where an expedition would include no females aboard ship). I was aghast that a science fiction reviewer would display such ignorance and folly in public. But, to him, because he suffers from a brain disease known as Liberalism or Progressivism or Leftism, any mention of sex which fails to portray women as equal if not superior to men is sexism. Even though my female main character is a superhuman being. And it is racism to portray non-Whites as superior to Whites because, um, that shows Whites are superior to non-Whites. (Okay, I am not clear on how anyone can look at a story which assumes each race as history turns will have its place in the sun, Babylonians, Greeks, Romans, Franks, Spaniards, English, ergo assumes no race is superior to any other... and cry racism. Maybe Mr. Braindead thought I meant to write a horror story, where portraying Hindus as being good at math and science scared me and my racist readers, sort of like *Planet of the Apes*?)

In other words, Progressives are required by their political brain disease to regard *everything* as propaganda. It is one of their dogmas that everything which is not pro-Progressive propaganda is reactionary and pro-evil propaganda. The braindead reviewer in this case was not able to see nor to imagine that I was writing a story which made no statement and took no position on the question of the equality of the races or the equality of the sexes. The idea that I the author might think the idea of an all-male expedition as a bad idea, or that the loss of Anglo-American values praising equality might be a bad idea, or that there is no racial difference between Portuguese and Spaniards, or whatever, simply never occurred to him. Again, the idea that I put something into my plot because the plot required it simply never occurred to him. The whole point of Progressivism is to train the brain to die in certain areas so that certain ideas simply cannot occur to you.

I call this a negative example because a reviewer saw a propagandist intent where none existed. The example shows that propaganda can always be seen when it is looked for, since all one need do it imagine something promotes a certain worldview (whether it does or not) and imagine that the worldview in question is an ideology (whether it is or not).

Here is the central problem with the question: all stories whether they like it or not have a moral. The moral of any story is always the winning behavior that leads to success in that story. In action-adventure stories, the moral is straightforward: courage and loyalty are good. In James Bond stories, the moral is that fast cars and hot women are good, and cool is good.

But if art is like life, and humans can glean morals from life, it is the moral-seeking behavior of the reader, not the moral preaching urge of the writer, that makes this part of storytelling universal.

At this point, I must hasten to say that all this discussion applies only to the social and political Right. We are able to read and write books that are not propaganda, because we can imagine a world outside the sphere of politics, and because we can imagine our fellow human beings as equals rather than as churls to be corrected, children to be instructed, disciples for a messiah to inspire, nor again as the passive patients of the social engineering efforts of enlightened experts.

Now, as with all things the modern socialist antinomian Left touches, storytellers are poisoned and ruined by Political Correctness, and so are story readers. The Leftist storyteller has no role in life except to tell propaganda, because the Leftist worldview holds all topics to be political, and all politics to be nothing but a Darwinian struggle for survival without honor, rules, let or quarter. The Leftist story reader is likewise ruined by Political Correctness, since it ruins his ability to see things. Instead of seeing things as they are, the Leftist sees things only as symbols for the Darwinian power struggle: hence, a story of self-sacrifice, such as when a hobbit suffers terribly to bring a magic ring to Mount Doom, is a symbol for Christianity which is a symbol for the oppression of women and therefore an enemy ; a hobbit is a symbol of the bourgeoisie and therefore an enemy; the friendship between Frodo and Sam is a symbol for an unexpressed desire for sodomy and therefore an enemy; orcs are symbols for Negros and therefore represent racism and therefore are an enemy. Frodo is not a woman, therefore this is a symbol displaying the hatred of women, and therefore everything is an enemy.

Symbols that are actually in the story, such as Sauron the Dark Lord being a type of Satan, or Smaug the dragon being an emblem of greed and hording, those symbols the Political Correctoid cannot see. Where you or I or any sane person might see and read a charming children's tale about the self-sacrifice of an inhabitant of Elfland trying to destroy a magic ring which otherwise will doom all the free peoples of Middle Earth, the Leftist sees nothing but enemies, vicious and demonic enemies, hellbent on the denigration and destruction of women, Negroes, and sodomites, and other weak, silly, mewling and helpless creatures the heroic Leftist must leap to defend… from the sinister menace of what, to you or me, is a children's story.

For the Left, all stories are propaganda for two reasons: (1) all stories read by Leftists can be deconstructed to be political tracts, including *Mary had a little lamb* because they have a brain disease which prevents them from seeing things as anything other than political symbols; (2) all the stories written by a self-consistent Leftist would be propaganda, since this is what their philosophy demands. Their philosophy demands that all things be political, because nothing exists but power relations. Fortunately, no self-consistent Leftist can actually exist in reality because self-consistency is inversely proportional to one's loyalty to Leftism, and so many people who worship at the shrines of Leftism on their Sabbath return to ordinary reality the other six days of the week, and some can do their jobs in an ordinary craftsman-like fashion, including the job of storytelling.

Let me return to the point above about one-sidedness. If a writer has an ax to grind, he must portray his bad guys as having no redeeming characteristics whatsoever, as with an Ayn Rand villain.

However, the writer will also portray his guys as lacking any redeeming characteristics when telling an action story or a space opera, because he wants the readers to cheer when the Death Star blows up, or when John Carter conquers the Martians, and not suffer sudden moral qualms about the widows and orphans created among the Stormtroopers or Green Martians.

An aside: Some reviewers dismiss Tolkien because he is seen as one-sided, that is, there are no orcs who sing songs and no elves that kick bunnies. But this is not true: the elves are as prone to pride and suspicion as anyone (see, for example, the scene where the Fellowship is captured and brought into Lothlorian) and even the orcs are portrayed as miserable under their slavery, and at least one yearns for the old days when he and his band could roam the hills and commit brigandage without overseers.

If a writer has an ax to grind, he need not give both sides of the story. And, in life, in every aspect of life except the highest (no one argues that good is bad, except Progressives) there is always a second side to consider (everyone argues about the priority or implementation of abstract goods into concrete policy, except progressives).

If a writer has an ax to grind, he will talk about the issues of the day, and not about eternal things. Dante is read today because of this talk about hell and heaven, which are still here, not his talk about Guelph and Ghibelline, which have passed away. Putting your ax to the grindstone pulls your eyes down from heaven and up from hell and places them firmly on matters that no one will care about in a generation.

For all this, some propaganda is unintentional. Repeating the ideals and ideas of better and more original writers, if you repeat their intent as well, makes you carry on propaganda without deliberately doing propaganda. Whenever a conservative commenter or Christian preacher says 'he or she' when the grammar rules call for 'he' he tacitly aids the cause of an ideology (called feminism) hellbent on destroying him, because he acts as if he agrees that grammar is innately a tool of oppression.

The best way to avoid propaganda in a story is for your art to impersonate life. Life is complex at times and simple at times. Some morals are clear (heroes should be brave) and some are debatable (governments should return to the gold standard). Some lend themselves easily to fiction, and some do not.

But propaganda, using the story to make a political point, cheats all readers outside the writer's narrow circle of fellow partisans. It puts the writer onstage in front of the puppet-show, rather than (where he should be) in the back, hidden, and pulling the strings, so that the children can applaud and cheer and scream when the little wooden dolls are changed by the magic of storytelling into heroes and princesses and monsters.

THE SILENT PLANET OF CS LEWIS

I HAD the opportunity to reread C.S. Lewis's *Out of the Silent Planet* and to see with adult and Christian eyes what first I read in my long-vanished and atheist youth.

This is the first of his famed 'Deep Heaven' Trilogy. Allow me to report that all three works are well worth rereading, and to argue that they are not merely good science fiction, but merit the top awards and accolades our beloved genre can bestow.

I have pondered patiently the argument often made that these works are not science fiction, and, fresh from immersion in them, I can now dismiss such arguments with profound yet deserved umbrage. To say that Lewis's works are not science fiction because they are Christian is the same as to say H.G. Wells' works are not science fiction because they are Socialist.

This article is written for those who have already read Lewis's Deep Heaven Trilogy. Spoilers abound.

Let me in the paragraphs below mention what makes a science fiction work great rather than mediocre; then remind the reader of some of the scenes and delights of Mr.

Lewis' inventive universe; perhaps with a meandering mention of the philosophical concerns or deeper questions Lewis lightly touches upon; in order to show that these are not merely good books, not merely good science fiction, but great.

But before any of this, let me mention the difference between reading a book as graybeard versus as a beardless boy.

The main difference is one of context. When I first read these books, I had not yet read either H.G. Wells' *First Men in the Moon*, nor Arthur C. Clarke's *Childhood's End*, and so did not see the connection between the three books. As an adult, I see parallels suggesting that Lewis in *Out of the Silent Planet* is writing a thematic rebuttal to Wells, and Clarke writes a rebuttal to Lewis.

A second contextual difference is that, as a youth, I was interested primarily in the sense of wonder of the science fiction elements of the story. Where C.S. Lewis touches on deeper concerns, I was too shallow then to follow the thought. Having been profoundly impressed by Lewis' nonfiction essays, particularly *The Abolition of Man*, my adult self sees when Lewis touches on a point, or the point, in his science fictional drama on a recurring theme from his nonfiction.

The final and most obvious contextual difference I notice now, writing in 2012 when America has just placed the Curiosity robot rover on the surface of Mars, is the assumption about how a Mars voyage could be made, particularly as a two-man expedition in an inventor's privately created bathysphere-shaped vehicle.

The assumption makes the book seem like an historical novel, which it did not seem to me when I first read it. The gulf of time between the reader and the writer did not exist, or, if it did, my youthful self was unaware of it.

Out of the Silent Planet was written in the years between
the First and Second World War, before the Manhattan
project, before jet aircraft, before the V-2 rocket, and before
the military-industrial complex and the idea of space travel
as a public works project. If the inventor in a book written in
those years was not the head of a government department of
science, and not the head of a major corporation, but instead
made his space flying vehicle in a shed behind his house,
keep in mind the only real historical example of that day and
age were men like the Wright Brothers, who did indeed make
their flying machine in a shed behind the bicycle shop, and
that their invention was only 35 years old at the time Mr.
Lewis wrote his book. That is roughly the same amount of
time between when the book was written, and when I read it
in the early 1970's.

The idea of a tinkerer with a private workshop, a la
Thomas Edison, inventing a space drive seems to us now as
quaint and absurd a conceit as climbing a plateau in South
America and finding dinosaurs. Quaint it might be, but it is
no more absurd than, in real life, Bill Gates cobbling together
a personal computer in his garage, or, in science fiction,
Professor Cavor constructing a space-travelling sphere of
antigravity alloy in his woodshed. *First Men in the Moon* is not
"Hard" SF of the fashion that Jules Verne or John W. Campbell Jr. preferred, but science fiction it certainly is, and it
would be absurd to argue otherwise.

This introduces the question of whether C.S. Lewis was
writing a real work of science fiction or merely some fantasy
that happened to be set in space as phantasmagorical and
unrealistic as *The Little Prince* by Antoine de Saint-Exupéry
or *Doctor Dolittle in the Moon* by Hugh Lofting.

Without dwelling on a tedious argument as to what
counts as real science fiction, I will start from the assumption that any definition of science fiction is worthless if it

rules out the most famous works of H.G. Wells, one of the three authors who can make a claim to have invented the genre (the other two being Jules Verne and the unfairly over-looked Olaf Stapledon).

Science fiction is the genre which introduces its sense of the fantastic through wonders made plausible by reference to the scientific worldview. In other words, science fiction has a setting, props, or characters of extraterrestrial or futuristic origins rather than magical or supernatural. A yarn set on Mars is science fiction, set in Oz is a fantasy; jetpack is science fiction, flying carpet is fantasy; a monster is fantasy, but a Morlock is science fiction.

Low-grade science fiction, space opera (my own genre) or sciffy (like *Star Wars*) use the props and settings but not the essential feature of the science fiction genre: The essential feature of science fiction is speculation from what is known to be scientifically plausible to what is implausible, to treat the unrealistic element in the tale realistically, so that the reader is taken as if by surprise: "Ah! Well, of course that is what it would be like!"

I use H.G. Wells as the example because he set the standard of the genre: when the evil scientist Gryphon in *The Invisible Man* throws off his coat, hat, dark glasses and face-bandages to turn invisible, rather than, like Bilbo in *The Hobbit* or Bradamant in *Orlando Furioso* using a magic ring, the unwarned (and unjaded) reader's reaction is one of surprise, almost recognition, when he realizes that a process which turns flesh and blood transparent would not turn clothing transparent. Bilbo is a fantasy character whereas Gryphon is a science fiction character precisely because Bilbo does not need to take off his clothes when invisible, nor wrap his face in bandages when visible.

Bilbo never once worries about leaving footprints in the snow when invisible, because this is precisely the kind of realistic detail which breaks the mood of fantasy and sets the mood of science fiction. If my magic ring turns my necktie invisible, what happens when I tuck the corner of the table cloth into my necktie and then put on the magic ring? Does everything I am touching turn invisible, including the chair in which I sit? Why not the carpet on which I stand? To ask such a question in a fantasy tale would break the mood and shatter the dream logic on which fantasy depends. To fail to ask such a question in a science fiction story is to fail to appeal to the science fiction reader's particular taste for treating unrealistic things realistically: because this is the one thing this genre has which none others do.

A werewolf story becomes science fictional (at least in mood) if the author bothers to mention the difference in weight between a man and a wolf, and he tells you what happens to the extra mass during the metamorphosis. The difference between science fiction and fantasy is not that fantasy has fantastic elements and science fiction has realistic ones. We have metamorphosis and invisibility and monsters and mind reading in science fiction just as much as in fantasy. The difference is that science fiction, in order to lend that extra atmosphere of verisimilitude, worries about the footprints of the invisible man; and our monsters are from outer space.

In *Out of the Silent Planet*, the scientist Weston invents a space-traveling sphere whose motive power is never told to the main character Ransom, nor to the reader, but merely said to rely on "exploiting the less observed properties of solar radiation." This is no more fantastical than the gravity-opaque alloy of professor Cavor in H.G. Wells' *First Men in the Moon*, and considerably less fantastical than the "back-rays" which propel the crystal-hulled space-traveling torpedo of David Lindsay in *Voyage to Arcturus*. In each case, the author was eager to carry his protagonists to an alien sphere, and did not dwell on the stage machinery of how to get there.

In none of the books is the vessel given a name. (Note that Jules Verne names the space gun Impey Barbacane uses to shoot a manned shell to the Moon, as well as naming the airship of Robur and the submersible of Nemo. Perhaps it is a rule that in "harder" SF stories the vehicles are characters in the stories, and merit names.)

The case against C.S. Lewis as a science fiction writer, if I understand it (and I confess I have never heard it articulated convincingly) rests on two points: the first is that the Christian religion is unambiguously a correct picture of the universe in his Deep Heaven Trilogy; the second is that his description of space flight is absurd.

Let us address this second point first, as it is the stronger point. C.S. Lewis makes an inexcusable gaffe, which no science fiction writer worth the name, even writing in 1938, should have made, when he asserts that the space-traveling sphere of Weston exerts a miniature gravity field, weaker than Earth's but still sufficient to pull objects to the deck and impart a clear vertical orientation.

From the description of crewmen sitting at chairs and eating from tables and washing up in the galley, the author is clearly describing gravity of at least lunar strength, perhaps between a fifth to a tenth of Earth's gravity. But the ship is not the size of Earth's moon. The center of the ship is not a chunk of neutronium nor an artificial gravity generator, but a hold where gear is stored. The men wear heavy weights to hold them to the floor. Perhaps Lewis was thinking of the lead belts of deep sea divers. But zero-gravity is not buoyancy. In reality, in a space capsule, such belts would do nothing, except increase one's inertia.

This gaffe is so egregious that until I reread it, I had not truly believed Lewis had made it. My memory of the book was that sphere contained the propulsive machinery, which somehow used the gravitic properties of solar radiation to produce artificial gravity inside the sphere and to produce thrust. But no. My childish mind had merely filled in details the author never mentions. Lewis does not say Weston's machine filters gravitons out of solar radiation; he only says some "less observed" properties are involved. My memory had tricked me. Nope, it was just a mistake, and an off-putting one, like going to a movie where a space captain uses 'parsecs' as a measure of time, not distance.

Lewis makes a similar gaffe when describing the close approach and landing of the space sphere. If the ship is under continual acceleration, the sensation of gravity would exist but only in the direction of motion; if not under acceleration, the ship is in free fall. Instead, Lewis makes an elementary, embarrassing error when he described the sphere approaching Mars and therefore the Martian gravity pulling the crew and their gear toward the one side of the sphere, which slowly becomes the "down" direction, but meanwhile the gravity pulling their bodies and gear toward the center of the sphere continues to operate, causing a confusion of the inner ear and of hand-eye coordination, so no one knows if he is holding a cup at lip level, or above, or below. The scene is imaginative, but based on a gross error of high school physics. Objects in free fall experience no gravity, as anyone who has ever survived a falling elevator can tell you, or para-chuted from an aeroplane. A man suspended between gravity sources, for example at right angles to each other, would be pulled toward the point of the vector sum, not be confused between two different sources of downwardness. That is, he would not feel that both the deck and the bulkhead were downward, he would just feel the deck was tilted at a forty-five degree angle.

And, like H.G. Wells, C.S. Lewis has his intrepid explorers

unscrew the wingnuts holding the ship's manhole cover-shaped hatch, and then take a deep breath of the (fortunately) breathable atmosphere. It is also fortunately at the same pressure as the ship, or else the hatch would have either exploded outward like a cork from a pop gun, or been as impossible to move as the lid of an hermetically sealed jar. Airlocks are apparently a postwar invention in science fiction. (Or even later. I am reminded of the similar scene from *Galaxy Quest* where Engineer Kwan dismounts from the airlockless shuttlecraft and tests the alien atmosphere by sniffing it.) Of course, Lewis deserves more credit than Wells, because he establishes that this is the explorer's second voyage to the world.

That said, in the same chapter which describes the flight through space, Lewis does the very opposite of a science gaffe. The pith of what science fiction writers do when they work their craft correctly is to describe imaginatively something which is a reasonable yet remarkable extrapolation of men in the extraordinary situation of the tale, and to do so vividly. Here he does it twice.

The first is his description of outer space as lit by a sun. It is one of those things obvious only in hindsight, because we on Earth are used to seeing the stars only at night, to assume that above the atmosphere, where the stars are, it is night. It is not: night is a local condition, a cone of shadow projected from the earth and extending no further than the orbit of the moon. In space, it is always noon (at least until you pass beyond Saturn or thereabouts).

But what Lewis does in addition is he makes the sunlight in space refreshing, reinvigorating, golden, almost spiritual, so that space is not merely 'outer space' but is 'Deep Heaven' crowded with a complex throng of unseen and perhaps angelic beings. In real life, Earth's atmosphere blocks forms of solar radiation dangerous to man; but the speculation that the atmosphere blocks beneficent rays as well was a perfectly valid science fictional speculation at the time.

At least, it is science fiction speculation no more outrageous than, say, the idea in 'Scanners Live in Vain' by Cordwainer Smith that space contains a radiation intensely painful to the human nervous system, or the idea in *First Men in the Moon* that travel through space induces a mystical sense of eternity and infinity–which is, no doubt, precisely where Lewis got the inspiration for the description of the golden and beatific light of Deep Heaven. Lewis is presenting something in mood and theme akin to a medieval and mythical view of celestial spaces, deliberately at odds with the stark inhumanity of H.G. Wells.

The second bit of science fictional craftsmanship is the description of the upper decks of the space sphere: namely, each bulkhead where the crewman stands seems perpendicular to the deck, but the far bulkhead on the opposite side of the cabin slants away. If he crosses to that bulkhead, it will seem perpendicular close at hand, but the one left behind now seems to slant away. And the overhead is larger than the deck, making the whole cabin wedge-shaped. This is the kind of clear and clever visual imagination of what it would really be like to live, in this case on a tiny wordlet, which many science fiction writers fail to mention. Other writers who set their stories inside O'Neill colonies, or Dyson Spheres or Ringworlds do not do as well in visualizing and helping the reader to visualize the unearthly environment.

I will not dwell on the description of the Martian life, intelligent and animal and vegetable, which Lewis lovingly and painstakingly describes, except to say that his surface of Mars, or Malacandra as the natives name it, is more vivid and memorable than H.G. Wells' description of the Lunar features inside and outside the Moon, and considerably more accurate given the scientific knowledge of the day.

(Wells has the Moon coated with a diurnal atmosphere, and covered with fungi that sprouts and blooms and dies once each fortnight. He places a liquid ocean inside the hollow volume of the Moon, and does not explain how the vast lunar sphere, if hollow, fails to collapse under its own weight.)

Lewis knew enough to know that the surface of Mars was uninhabitable, frozen with subarctic temperatures, and that if there were canals on Mars, to be visible on Earth they would have to be canyons of immense width, and, if as straight as Percival Lowell described, artificial. He places the atmosphere and ecology, fed by hot springs to give it Earth-like temperatures, within these canals. And he makes the deadliness of the outer surface above the canals the wounds of an ancient and superscientific or supernatural war between Malacandra and our world, Thulcandra, which gives the whole conceit a grandeur and mythic weight any writer should envy.

A science fiction writer of ordinary imagination might, as Lewis did, give his Martians the great stature, thin legs and wide, birdlike chests to be expected of a world of less than earthly gravity; but it takes a particular cleverness of the science fictional imagination to describe the waves of water as being taller and thinner than Earthly eyes expect, or the dizzying narrowness of hills and mountains, and then to express these unearthly imaginings as hauntingly beautiful despite their strangeness.

The Earthman's landing on Mars is strikingly memorable, because Ransom, at first, cannot comprehend the Martian landscape, or tell land from water. It then takes a science fiction writer of more than ordinary philosophical under-standing to realize, as Lewis did, that a man dropped on an alien planet for the first time would not be able to distin-guish what the colored shapes and textures around him represented, whether water or cloud or mountain or oddity of unknown treelike growth. Surely an earthly forest, seen from afar, would be mistaken for a strangely-textured sponge, or a cloud catching the sunlight at the wrong angle be seen as an odd mountain on the horizon made of gold and ivory, when first beheld by a man from Mars.

Lewis then uses a conceit so original for its time that many a science fiction writer after him copied it without hesitation. The idea is that a truly advanced race would live in Edenic simplicity, and be mistaken by blundering explorers at first for savages, the irony being that the explorers themselves are savages. I have seen this conceit done a number of times, but one of the more famous is the episode of *Star Trek* episode "Errand of Mercy" where the Organians, who seem at first to live at a medieval level of technology, are actually energy beings of immeasurably vast powers, almost godlike.

It is perfectly valid science fictional speculation asking what would happen if a world, unlike Earth, was peopled by races as intelligent as man, but not as immoral as man, or, to use a theological term, not fallen.

An even cleverer speculation appears only in the post-script, where the protagonist mentions that the three intelligent races of Mars do not keep pets: they have no emotional need to treat dogs and cats and horses almost like people, because the oddness and humor and fellowship we seek outside our species and find in pets, they find in the other two intelligent species.

All this, and many more examples besides, show that C.S. Lewis handles the material of science fiction adequately with his peers in the science fiction field. I next assert that his writing is superior and for three reasons: first, his use of the English language shows more craft and skill.

His writing is simply better and more evocative of mood

and visual images than writers like Arthur C. Clarke or Isaac Asimov. I would compare the evocative look and detail of the Martians described by C.S. Lewis, for example, to the Martians from Robert Heinlein, except that there is nothing aside from a few provocative adverbs to hint at their appearance.

H.G. Wells does a better job, but upon rereading, I note that he does not actually describe what it looks like. Allow me to quote at length in order to make my point:

A big greyish rounded bulk, the size, perhaps, of a bear, was rising slowly and painfully out of the cylinder. As it bulged up and caught the light, it glistened like wet leather. Two large, dark-coloured eyes were regarding me steadfastly. The mass that framed them, the head of the thing, was rounded, and had, one might say, a face. There was a mouth under the eyes, the lipless brim of which quivered and panted, and dropped saliva. The whole creature heaved and pulsated convulsively. A lank tentacular appendage gripped the edge of the cylinder, another swayed in the air. Those who have never seen a living Martian can scarcely imagine the strange horror of its appearance. The peculiar V-shaped mouth with its pointed upper lip, the absence of brow ridges, the absence of a chin beneath the wedge-like lower lip, the incessant quivering of this mouth, the Gorgon groups of tentacles, the tumultuous breathing of the lungs in a strange atmosphere, the evident heaviness and painfulness of movement due to the greater gravitational energy of the earth—above all, the extraordinary intensity of the immense eyes—were at once vital, intense, inhuman, crippled and monstrous. There was something fungoid in the oily brown skin, something in the clumsy deliberation of the tedious movements unspeakably nasty.

Nightmarish, certainly. But what does it look like? A brain with tentacles? A squid? A man with a big head? Does it have four limbs or more? A bipedal stance?

And, unlike Lewis, we know nothing of their psychology,

society, or anything of the Wellsian Martians. The noble Hrossa of Malacandra have a quite different voice and manner than, say the solemn Sorn or the wry Pfifltriggi. In contrast, the Martians of Robert Heinlein are asexual and patient as Ents. None has a personality. The Martians of H.G. Wells are merely monsters.

In the postscript mentioned above, the narrator describes the haunting scene of seeing Jupiter rising like the evening star, and hearing the deep and solemn choir of the Martians ringing out to it, in words unknown, and hailing it as the throne of the heavens. Because, after all, despite the temptation to write science fiction in the clipped and angular style of Earnest Hemmingway or a wireless newspaper report, we are supposed to evoke emotion through the craft and beauty of language, and to be, if only in a small way, poets. The scenes should be remembered, and be more than memorable. They should be haunting.

Second, Lewis is simply a better writer than H.G. Wells when it comes to conveying personality, humor, or a convincing vividness. I feel I have met Ransom. I can tell you more of the personality and person of Weston than I can of Cavor, and much more about Devine than Bedford.

Third, Lewis touches upon deeper issues, philosophical and theological, which only the most ambitious art aspires to. Lewis moves like an expert swimmer in these profound depths. If you have ever read a science fiction author trying to be profound when he has nothing deep to say, such as, say, Robert Heinlein in *Have Space Suit Will Travel*holding that the genocide of whole species who show a warlike nature is morally licit, you get the impression of men treading water and grasping at straws.

Compare this to the theophany at the climax of *Out of the Silent Planet*. In this scene, the planetary intelligence of Mars, having heard the typical cant of manifest destiny and eugenic

Darwinism so popular among intellectuals between the wars, saying that higher species of men should wipe out the lower, coming from the mouth of Weston, says that Weston's moral code, like all allegedly modern moral codes, is merely a corruption of the general and universal moral maxims all men know by intuition.

Again, allow me to quote at length:

"Tell him," said Weston when he had been made to understand this, "that I don't pretend to be a metaphysician. I have not come here to chop logic. If he cannot understand—as apparently you can't either—anything so fundamental as a man's loyalty to humanity, I can't make him understand it."

But Ransom was unable to translate this and the voice of Oyarsa continued:

"I see now how the lord of the silent world has bent you. There are laws that all hnau (rational creatures) know, of pity and straight dealing and shame and the like, and one of these is the love of kindred. He has taught you to break all of them except this one, which is not one of the greatest laws; this one he has bent till it becomes folly and has set it up, thus bent, to be a little, blind Oyarsa in your brain. And now you can do nothing but obey it, though if we ask you why it is a law you can give no other reason for it than for all the other and greater laws which it drives you to disobey. Do you know why he has done this?"

Weston replies that he is a modern man, and does not believe that old talk of morality and rubbish. The Oyarsa continues:

"I will tell you. He has left you this one because a bent hnau can do more evil than a broken one. He has only bent you; but this Thin One who sits on the ground he has broken, for he has left him nothing but greed. He is now only a talking animal and in my world he could do no more evil than an animal. If he were mine I would unmake his body, for the hnau in it is already dead. But if you were mine I would try to cure you.

As I child, I would not have noticed how quickly and adroitly CS Lewis touches on and uses these two central concerns that he dwells in his brilliant non-fiction essays, especially *The Abolition of Man*.

As an adult, I notice that the whole scene where Ransom is translating into the true and honest speech of the Malacandrans the cant and jargon of the modern intellectual, and showing (with subtle satire on Lewis' part) that it is either meaningless, or it is diabolical: merely fancy words to cover up the true nature of the criminal intent.

The second man, the Thin One, mentioned above is Devine, who is not a scientist but a businessman. Lewis was copying closely his model from *First Men in the Moon*, and Devine is his Bedford, a businessman, the way Weston is his Cavor, a scientist. Like the Spaniards in the New World, Devine's interest is the gold the natives possess in abundance. He serves no real purpose in the plot, but he does exist to make exactly this point, which is a point characteristic of Christian writers. The great are more prone to great harm; Lucifer was not the least of the angels in heaven, but the brightest.

As for the general background of the solar system setting, it is actually quite elegant, even brilliant. Every world has a superior being or Eldil associated with it or assigned to it. Unbeknownst to Earthlings, except as legend, the ruling planetary intelligence of Earth flew into rebellion against his peers, and these superior beings in retaliation isolated and besieged the world. No messages cross Deep Heaven to or from the Earth, which is called Thulcandra, the Silent Planet. The beings have communion with other worlds, and know who and what dwells there, both mortal and immortal, physical and not: but not of Earth.

The resonance with the tale of the Fall of Lucifer is, of course, deliberate, but one misses the whole point of how eerie the concept is if one fails to see it through science fiction eyes, and therefore to see it afresh. The paradox of why we have not been visited by superior beings or extraterrestrial races if such races are commonplace in the cosmos has an easy, if creepy, explanation. Earth is a cross between a quarantined leper colony and a dark-faced fortress beleaguered by foes, and we are as ignorant of the dark yet superhuman forces secretly ruling our world as Neo was ignorant of the Matrix before he swallowed the red pill.

The second argument that Lewis is not an SF writer is that Christianity is incompatible with the scientific worldview needed as a backdrop for science fiction. This is again an argument I have never heard well-articulated, and until I hear it well articulated, I doubt it worthy of attention. The idea of portraying the themes and symbols of Christianity in a science fiction background is certainly as original as H.G. Wells portraying the universe as hopeless and horrible, or Robert Heinlein portraying the universe as a backdrop for orgies and genocides.

The whole point of science fiction is that the conceit that we actually know what the universe is actually like is conceited. All science fiction contains a hint of that dizzying truth that truth is stranger than we imagine. And nothing could be stranger for a science fiction reader to find that the lore he learned at his mother's knee and despised in college and forgot among his worldly cares is not only dazzling truth, but the merest corner of an unimaginable glory that opens depth upon depth into a deepest heaven.

Or is it the morality of Christianity that is said to be unscientific? That is the kind of argument we have not heard since the 1930's, when the advocates of Eugenics were shamed into silence by the visible manifestations of the horrors they preached. Science fiction as a whole is certainly not wedded to the type of grotesque and infantile moral code advocated by people who excuse hedonism, cruelty, abortion, human experimentation, mass murder and other gross degradations of human dignity in the name of science.

Nor can morality be left out of science fiction altogether. All good science fiction stories have a moral mood and atmosphere, a metaphysical background as well as a counter-factual physics.

For example, H.G. Wells in *First Men in the Moon* took the assumption of Darwinism and applied it to the insectoid denizens of the Moon: they are bred and conditioned to their tasks and stored in a drugged stupor until needed. This is the first, and still one of the most chilling and fascinating portrayals of an inhuman hivelike society so popular in dystopian science fiction. Wells is an adroit enough writer to show both the good and bad side of the moon-sized termite mound, for his Selenites have neither war nor commercial competition, and are so shocked when they discover from Cavor that mankind indulges in these unimaginable evils, in order to quarantine the Earth, they kill him. The Grand Lunar never pays for this crime, nor is it clear that the sympathies of the author or reader are not meant to be with him.

The parallel scene in *Out of the Silent Planet* has the Oyarsa of Mars command the Earthlings to return to Earth, a remarkably dangerous journey given that the planets are no longer in conjunction, and the superbeing programs (or ordains) the space vessel to evaporate in a flash of energy within ninety days, whether the men have reached ground or not. The superior being has power enough, the least of his servants could do so, to destroy any additional space vessels leaving the atmosphere of Earth. Ransom makes it out of the vessel after landing just in time, like Lot escaping Sodom as it burns.

In order to prevent Bedford from making any sequel

voyages into space, H.G. Wells, in a fashion I can only describe as ghoulish, has a small boy discover the space sphere after Bedford lands on Earth and crawls away from it, and stepping innocently or mischievously inside, the nameless boy accidentally closes the antigravity shutters, and is thrown into space to die of starvation or strangulation, weeping and screaming, weightless as in an endless fall down a bottomless pit, with no body for his searching parents to discover. Bedford never tells the parents, or the police, the fate of the missing boy. The moral atmosphere thus portrayed is one of utterly appalling inhumanity, almost akin to a horror story: two men voyage to the Moon and one of them is captured, cross examined, and killed by bugs. The other returns to earth and looses his space machine when it accidentally kills a child. I submit that if this is a proper moral and metaphysical backdrop for a science fiction story, the awe and wonder and fundamentally positive view portrayed in Lewis' writings are just as good a backdrop, and, for anyone aside from disaffected adolescents, considerably more edifying.

Childhood's End is written as a rebuttal to Lewis, as if to prove that the scientific progress of the human race could lead to spiritual development. I do not propose that this was any conscious intent of Arthur C. Clark: I merely point out that the two books deal with the same theme from opposite directions. In *Childhood's End* space aliens of immense superiority, who just so happen to look like cartoon devils, arrive on earth, impose a benevolent tyranny to prevent wars and cruelty to animals, in the hopes that the next generation of men will be a more evolved species, have psychic powers, and be too intelligent for men to understand.

And so it proves: mankind withers under the psychologically inescapable burden of realizing that all religions are false and that their children are non-human; they cease to reproduce, and politely step aside into Darwinian extinction to allow the Homo Superiors elbow room. (Magneto would have been pleased with their graciousness.) The superchildren then dissolve the Earth into nothingness, and achieve a oneness with a Cosmic Overmind which is as near to the Gnostic myths of a return to the Pleorma as science fiction can imagine. The pure intellectuals, or, to be blunt, invisible angels into which the children of men evolve go flittering away among the stars and dance on the head of a pin. There is no doctrine of the resurrection of the body in Arthur C Clarke's book.

Those who argue that the eldil and Oyarsa of C.S. Lewis are nothing but angels and archangels, and, as such, put his writing outside the scope of science fiction, I will only nod toward the writing of Olaf Stapledon, who has not angels but God Almighty as a character in his book STARMAKER, and toward the Organians of *Star Trek* and the Cosmic Overmind of *Childhood's End*, or countless other beings made of energy or pure thought who people the worlds of science fiction in countless swarms, to make that assertion absurd.

The whole point of Lewis' depiction of the Eldil is to find a being of greater power than man, made of no substance he recognizes, which does not clearly fit into the category of either myth or science, categories Lewis in writings both fiction and nonfiction wonders may be arbitrary (or at least earthly rather than universal). Lewis treats with the angels in the same way science fiction authors treat anything: as a speculation. He wonders what the superior beings would look like if encountered in outer space, or, rather, in Deep Heaven.

In other words, I would turn the same argument on its head: the fact that in a science fiction story by C.S. Lewis he puts Angels on Mars no more disinherits the book from the classification of science fiction than numberless other authors putting Men on Mars.

In sum, C.S. Lewis is not merely a good science fiction writer, as his speculations and imaginations of voyages through space and life on other worlds show. He demonstrates a poetical command of the language, an ability to provoke hauntingly striking images and ideas, an ability to portray personality and humor, and he shows a concern for deeper themes than typical for the genre: and this makes him not merely a good craftsman at his craft, but great.

9

VOYAGE TO VENUS BY CS LEWIS

I HAD the opportunity to reread PERELANDRA, the second in C.S. Lewis' Deep Heaven Trilogy. As I mentioned in my previous column on *Out of the Silent Planet*, Lewis' first in that trilogy, it is interesting to note the difference reading it as a youth compared to as a greybeard. I will report that the change is entirely favorable. As I grew, the book got bigger.

As with the previous article, I write for readers who have read the Deep Heaven Trilogy, so spoilers abound. Wise readers will read the book before reading this essay. You are warned.

Of the various experiences which changed my view on *Perelandra*, the smallest change was due to my conversion. In other words, if any atheist reader of mine is worried that the alleged Christian propaganda of the work is so cloying it will stick in his throat, all I can say is that I was likely a fiercer atheist then than you are now, and it did not stick in mine.

Again, I can assure my Christian readers that there are the typical trenchant insights of Lewis into the human condition and the divine nature all fans of his come to expect, if you look for them; but they are not intrusive if you are not looking for them. And I take this ability to offer to each reader what he wants and no more, to be a sign of a superior author.

This makes me conclude that, like *Out of the Silent Planet*, the book is actually a better book of science fiction qua science fiction than those who sit in the seats of the scornful are likely to admit. The Christian apologetic of the book, or what there is of it, is not the main appeal.

The greatest change in my own viewpoint across the years is the change from an inability to see the work in context compared to the other works of science fiction before and after it. In this respect, allow me to dwell on merely two books: *The Time Machine* by H.G. Wells and *A Voyage to Arcturus* by David Lindsay. I am convinced that Lewis was consciously copying themes and ideas and inspirations from these books.

I wonder if the book's other title, *Voyage to Venus*, was chosen in homage to David Lindsay's novel?

I had in the days of my distant youth read David Lindsay's *A Voyage to Arcturus*, while in no way understanding the heavily-disguised symbolic point of that strangely haunted, abundantly imaginative, and ultimately nihilistic work, nor did I see, in my robust innocence of mind, the moral degradation and despair of Lindsay. I did not know that Lewis had also read it, nor how he admired the same strengths I had. Rereading *Perelandra*, I now see parallelism strongly reminiscent of Lindsay's work in Lewis. It is an homage, if not a rebuttal to Lindsay.

As to whether or not the book counts as Science Fiction, it would be peremptory of me to dismiss all arguments claiming *Perelandra* is not Science Fiction by characterizing them as arguments about nothing but whether the book is science fiction of the type one likes: but I am strongly tempted.

Perelandra is not "Hard" SF after the fashion of Jules Verne or John W. Campbell Jr's stable of writers. Those who define Science Fiction narrowly enough to exclude H.G. Wells and everything not printed in Analog Magazine, I need not trouble myself to answer. It is sufficient for my purposes that we include *Perelandra* in the same genre as *The Time Machine* or *Voyage to Arcturus*. If you consider these not to be science fiction, so be it; but if you find them in the bookstore, tell me in which section you find them.

I will say that Soft SF is characterized by an emphasis on the human aspects of the story, on themes and philosophical statements, and is less interested in making solidly rooted speculations about realistic future or extraterrestrial technology. Hard SF is speculation for the mind; Soft SF is speculation for the heart.

What Soft SF, or much of it, is trying to do is convey to an earthly reader what a voyage to another world remote in space or time would be like, would feel like, and how it would change us, rather than concerned with the realism of the machinery to take us there.

Indeed, Soft SF is notorious for how casually it treats the stage-machinery which carries the narrative to another era or another world. The Time Machine of H.G. Wells' unnamed Time Traveler is described as a glittering metallic framework of nickel, ivory and brass, larger than a bicycle, with a bar of oddly twinkling "unreal" looking transparent crystalline substance in the works. Aside from this briefest of nods to the idea that time is fourth dimension which can be crossed much as a balloon allows a man to ascend in the vertical dimension, the Time Machine is a piece of stage machinery no more scientifically explicable than the Ghost of Christmas Future: merely a prop to get the narrative to the year 802701 A.D.

Likewise, in *A Voyage to Arcturus*, the oddly named protagonist Maskull is transported by what is perhaps the least convincing vehicle of all scientifictiondom: a torpedo-shaped car or carriage of crystal pulled by a container of liquefied "back-rays" from Arcturus, improbably described as that form of light which returns to its source. Cyrano flying to the moon by means of standing on an iron plate and throwing a magnet moon-ward, catching it and throwing it again as the plate rises, is in comparison positively Arthur-cclarkean.

Dr. Ransom's voyage is in a container also crystalline, this one suggestively (albeit quite reasonably) shaped like a coffin, and carried from England across the deeps to Perelandra by an "eldil", which is an invisible energy-being or angel inhabiting what mortals think of as empty outer space. Ransom during the voyage is in a state of suspended animation, or, rather a state which is above normal animation as hibernation is below it, some sort of timelessness suggestive of unity with eternal things rather than suggestive of, say, Buck Rogers unconscious and unaging due to radioactive gas.

However, for all its casual treatment of scientific realism, I will assert that Soft science fiction still takes place in the science fiction setting, that is, it is a science fiction story and not a ghost story nor a detective story nor a pirate story nor a mainstream novel, and as such it is obligated not to offend any known principle or fact of science. The Time Traveler of H.G. Wells is free to travel into some future world where, absurdly, the class distinctions of English gentry and work-ingmen are the primary factor in Darwinian evolution to produce cannibal troglodyte Morlocks and hapless Eloi, because as unlikely as this voyage and destination are, when the Time Traveler arrives, the world is not flat, nor does the sun rise in the West, nor does he encounter the battle of Armageddon and the New Jerusalem, but instead encounters evolution, entropy, giant crabs, and decay. No matter how unlikely, the Morlock world is still science fiction, because it is one of the most striking mythical images of the scientific viewpoint of time, namely, the appalling immensity of geologic ages which do not have mankind as their center.

What makes *The Time Machine* a science fiction tale is not the science fact but the science myth. And by "myth" I do not here mean a false story, I mean a symbol which has both emotional power and mental clarity. Namely, the myth or symbol that Man is no more privileged than the dinosaurs to be free from the remorseless Darwinian grinding-machinery of time.

In *Perelandra*, Ransom arrives on a Venus no more in keeping with modern scientific knowledge of that hellishly hot and poison-smothered sphere than the advent of John Carter on Barsoom is in keeping with modern knowledge of the surface conditions of Mars.

Or, I should say rather, that the modern knowledge of the surface conditions of Mars and Venus places the work of Isaac Asimov and Robert Heinlein in that same Nevernever-land of worlds which, at one time, were not scientifically impossible, but which in the current decade are. The Mars appearing in *Stranger in a Strange Land* or *Double Star* is no more scientifically credible than the oceanic Venus haunted by telepathic fish described in Isaac Asimov's *Lucky Star* books, nor the swampy Venus inhabited by intelligent dinosaurs described in Heinlein's *Between Planets* nor the venereal Las Vegas of *Podkayne of Mars*. But all these books are science fiction, no matter how badly dated the science is. Call them retrofuture fiction, if you insist, but it is hardly a strike against the author that real science could not keep pace with all the fascinating developments in make-believe.

At one time, the scientific consensus was that Mars was an older world and Venus younger than Earth. This led to a natural consensus about the stories to be set on Mars and

Venus: namely, that Mars was a dying world of dead sea bottoms covered with ancient ruins of a scientifically advanced civilization, and Venus was the hot and swampy haunt of dinosaurs and cavegirls in smilodon-skin bikinis, primitive and savage. And everyone from H.G. Wells to Edgar Rice Burroughs to Clarke Ashton Smith to C.L. Moore followed this consensus view.

And here I should mention that this is the second change of viewpoint which influenced the book in my eyes. When I first read it, it was still within the bounds of scientific possibility that Venus, under her eternal clouds, might hold an earthlike or semi-earthlike atmosphere. As an adult, I can only look on these retrofuturistic speculations with the avuncular indulgence one uses in studying sketches for Victorian steam-powered heavier-than-air craft. Ironically, a man in the age of nuclear submarines cannot read Jules Verne with the same attention and affection that he can read H.G. Wells. The *Nautilus* of Verne, because it is a prediction that came to pass, no longer has the glamor of the unknown hanging about it; whereas the antigravity sphere of Cavor, flying to a moon with an atmosphere inhabited by intelligent and inhuman termites, still has some mythic power to move the imagination. The Softer science fiction, by being less realistic, has a longer shelf life.

For that reason, here again, C.S. Lewis excels above his genre material and tropes: a man could just as easily be carried in a crystal space coffin by energy-angels now in 2011 as in 1943. Because he is trying to make a true myth with some philosophical depth to it, the work will remain of interest to readers for so long as poetry, song, philosophy, and wonder are of interest to civilized men.

It is to C.S. Lewis' credit that he takes this consensus view of the science fiction planets and turns them to his own purpose of making a deeper point about the nature of life and death, primitive and advanced, time and destiny. For example, the mortals of Malacandra express surprise at the idea that any race should depart its home world to seek another if that home were dying: for like Stoics do, they have no fear of death, and they hope for life beyond this one as Christians do (or, for that matter, as do the Martians in *Stranger in a Strange Land* and the Arisians in *Children of the Lens*.)

More interesting is the way in which the concept itself of "other worlds" is used by C.S. Lewis. It is worth quoting in full:

Tormance [the fictional world orbiting Arcturus in Lindsay] is a region of the spirit. He [David Lindsay] is the first writer to discover what 'other planets' are really good for in fiction. No merely physical strangeness or merely spatial distance will realize that idea of otherness which is what we are always trying to grasp in a story about voyaging through space: you must go into another dimension. To construct plausible and moving 'other worlds' you must draw on the only real 'other world' we know, that of the spirit.

Ransom does arrive on a Venus, which changes him in profound and subtle ways, much as the traveler in *A Voyage to Arcturus* is changed. And the change is not physical. Venus is another world spiritually, not just physically. If any writer other than David Lindsay and C.S. Lewis attempted so ambitious a depiction, I am unaware of it.

Nor do I think it too outrageous to say that, in my judgment, Lewis succeeds where Lindsay fails.

Lindsay in *A Voyage to Arcturus* is attempting to project the moral and spiritual atmosphere of a crooked Gnostic myth, a combination of Nietzschean ambition, Stoic fortitude, and solemn Neoplatonic mysticism. As such the author leads his protagonist Maskull from one symbolic meeting to another to another: each one allegorical landscape contains roughly one character for everyone chapter, each character representing one competing philosophy, which is each time shown to fall short of Lindsay's Promethean vision. The end result is flat despair: the world of Tormance, and by extension all human life in the mortal sphere, is declared to be worthless, merely a deception.

By contrast, C.S. Lewis has a more wholesome view both of material and spiritual life, and, as a Christian, I am allowed to say it is the more realistic view, the closer to truth. As such, Lewis' protagonist need not meet a stiff series of characters, one per chapter, to make his point. He need only contrast the landscape of Perelandra with its one inhabitant, the Green Lady (who, like the wife of Adam in Genesis, is not given a name until after the drama's finale) as the wholesome spirit, and the bent eldil inhabiting Weston as the unwholesome. For a Christian, there is only wise obedience to the highest good and the temptation to be disobedient, selfish, stupid.

I am also willing to assert that Lewis succeeds in something none of the 'consensus' writers (with the possible exception of Edgar Rice Burrough's Amtor) manages to achieve: he gives the consensus view of Venus as a primitive world a personality and a spirit of her own.

He does this by a daring means no other science fiction writer would attempt. His background conceit for the solar system, or "the Field of Arbol" is that myths and legends on Earth have been subtly or overtly influenced by the immortal energy beings of Deep Heaven, so that what old stories and medieval images say about Mars and Venus are true, if seen as in a glass darkly. Mars, the Roman War-God, partakes of the masculine nature of the Oyarsa called Malacandra, even as the voluptuous goddess Venus is a distorted and earthly reflection of the sublime pleasures of Perelandra. Throughout, Lewis uses heraldic images and mythic references to make the world of Venus seems as familiar to us as some half-forgotten story from Ovid or Spencer. But to this he adds the eye of a science fiction writer to give the world a striking and memorable appeal to the visual imagination.

While there are dragons, there are no dinosaurs on Lewis' Venus, but then again his notion of what a primitive world might be was far different from, say, the modern for whom the word primitive means unevolved and barbaric.

Venus is Eden; and the star of the Hesperides is the garden of Hesperides.

In one of the more memorable passages, Venus is said to be the younger world of the SF consensus in another sense of youth: it is spiritually younger, that is, the epochs of life on Mars and Tellus have been superseded. The condition of Venus does not allow for beast-shaped intelligent life, since the Incarnation on Tellus changed forever what form intelligence must have. Life must hereafter resemble the Creator more and more closely. The Perelandrans are also to be placed in a superior station to the Eldil or angels; and hence the fall of that world's first parents, should they and their world fall in darkness, would be immeasurably worse than the fall of Adam and Eve. This is because the younger world is a more ambitious project by the Creator.

Venus is also a world of pleasure. The description of the exquisite pleasures of eating fruit or drinking water have a haunting profundity to them, for the author is describing a spiritual change in Ransom which goes hand in hand with his eating of the unearthly food, or being showered by the unearthly waters.

What makes this an act of towering imagination, is that Lewis envisions for us, and describes, what it must be like to experience to enjoy intense sensual pleasure *innocently*. Unless my readers are utterly unlike me, the idea of a pleasure both innocent and sensual is rare. The unwillingness of Ransom to repeat or seek those pleasures, and yet to welcome them all the more when they come, is the unusual speculation of what an utterly non-hedonistic epicurean would be like: to the Earthly reader, this is a merely paradox, an impossibility.

But the central theme of *Perelandra*, emphasized by the symbolism of a world of floating islands which move as the spirit moves them, tossed by wind and wave under no mortal control of sail or rudder, is one of Edenic innocence. In the oceans of paradise, what is there to fear, no matter which way the wind blows? Where is there to go that is not fair? Even as the floating islands of Venus move hither and yon, submissive to the will of the waves, so too are the unfallen King and Queen of that remote world as trusting of the future Providence intends for them, without any impulse to be selfish, grasping, fearful, or disobedient.

Lindsay in *Voyage to Arcturus* has a similar theme, that is, each time the Earthly sojourner there eats the food of Tormance, some change of outlook, inevitably a new deception by the Demiurge, overwhelms the protagonist. It happens to Ransom only once: he bites into seaweed, and suddenly sees and understands the viewpoint of the mysterious undersea denizens of that world, to whom the world of the surface, the human world, is as remote to them as the high clouds of a winter sky.

Certain other visual images had that same striking Tormance mood in Lewis as can be found in Lindsay, such as the image of the solitary mountain in an otherwise sea-covered world whose peaks penetrate the golden clouds of the roof. For that matter, portraying the endless sky-roof of the fogs of Venus as the warm gold of old paintings is just as visually imaginative. And I recall no other author mentioning the realistic sounding and visually striking detail of the shining webs of reflected sea-waves dancing over the fogbanks far overhead like the bright rectilinear shadows which play off the ceiling of an indoor swimming pool. And again, there are crystal caves and mountains of glass and seascapes of floating isles, brightly colored as tropical birds, lovingly described.

One particular description struck my memory and left a deep impression, that I must quote it in full:

...He came to a new kind of vegetation. He was approaching a forest of little trees whose trunks were only about two and a half feet high; but from the top of each trunk there grew long streamers which did not rise in the air but flowed in the wind downhill and parallel to the ground. Thus, when he went in among them, he found himself wading knee-deep and more in a continually rippling sea of them—a sea which presently tossed all about him as far as his eye could reach. It was blue in colour, but far lighter than the blue of the turf—almost a Cambridge blue at the centre of each streamer, but dying away at their tasselled and feathery edges into a delicacy of bluish grey which it would take the subtlest effects of smoke and cloud to rival in our world. The soft, almost impalpable, caresses of the long thin leaves on his flesh, the low, singing, rustling, whis-pering music, and the frolic movement all about him, began to set his heart beating with that almost formidable sense of delight which he had felt before in Perelandra. He realised that these dwarf forests —these ripple trees as he now christened them—were the explana-tion of that water-like movement he had seen on the farther slopes.

When he was tired he sat down and found himself at once in a new world. The streamers now flowed above his head. He was in a forest made for dwarfs, a forest with a blue transparent roof, continually moving and casting an endless dance of lights and shades upon its mossy floor.

Now here is a test for your science fictional imagination. Without looking on the Internet or any other source mate-rial to prompt your memory, can you call to mind a vegetable from another planet?

(For the record, I myself can think of a few: the living wooden starships of *Hyperion* by Dan Simmons, the cabbage-like plant the boys spend the night under in Heinlein's *Red Planet*, the moss of Barsoom, the towering jungles from *Hothouse* by Brian W Aldiss, the glassy-leaved trees of the Lusion Plain from Lindsay's *Voyage to Arcturus*, or the endlessly fecund animal-trees of Matterplay)

I assure you that if you can bring such an image quickly to mind, the author who invented an unearthly tree has done his work as a science fiction author, and planted (no pun intended) in your imagination a world that is not real but which seems real.

The final perspective I saw upon rereading as an adult was the parallels to H.G. Wells *The Time Machine*. There are thematic, but I am convinced Lewis had Wells in mind.

First, there is the framing sequence. *Out of the Silent Planet* uses that most hoary and beloved but not even remotely convincing conceit that the author is merely the editor of some manuscript or transcriber of an interview given by the extraterrestrial adventurer.

Now, of course, since I, John C. Wright, was once contacted by Neil Armstrong and told in strictest confidence the true and astonishing adventures of that intrepid astronaut among the Catwomen of the Moon and how he rescued their fair yet furry Princess Miao-ro-Na from the Glass Labyrinth of the immense and weightless Space-Spider from the Unlife Zone at the Moon's dark core, I think of the idea of an adventurer telling his story immediately to an obscure midlist science fiction writer much more likely than telling, you know, the press and the scientific community. Until now the Official Secrets Act and the skepticism of an unwitting public has required me to withhold the fantastic details, and while it is true that Mr. Armstrong told me this story shortly after his return from the moon, um, when I was eight years old—

You get my point. The idea that C.S. Lewis is hurriedly writing down the space traveling adventures of his good friend and college don J.R.R. Tolkien who was kidnapped by Oppenheimer and Howard Hughs and carried off an experimental space vessel in 1938, and that Lewis is writing up an faithful account of Tolkien's advent on Mars, just changing the names, as in *Dragnet*, to protect the innocent, would not fool a child.

Be that as it may, in the postscript to *Out of the Silent Planet*, the narrator (the diegetic version of C.S. Lewis) hints darkly that the next adventure of the eldils touching the Silent Planet of Earth will be in time rather than through space. This hint is somewhat realized in *Perelandra*, if it is taken as a voyage to an Eden, which, while current on Venus, to an Earthman is a thing of the past.

Both in *The Time Machine* and *Perelandra*, the voyager has no physical evidence of his trip aside from an unearthly flower. In both tales, both travelers land in what seems a paradise, albeit the paradise of Perelandra turns out to be true. Both battle subterranean menaces in the dark, Morlocks in one case, and the Un-Man in the other. In Wells, the Time Traveler looks sick and careworn to the narrator, whereas in Lewis the Space Traveler is so robust and filled with superhuman health, the narrator looks sick to him. Both tell their tale to the diegetic narrator over a meal, albeit with the highly symbolic difference. In Wells, it is a dinner, as befits a tale of the death of a world. In Lewis, it is a breakfast as befits a world being born. The Time Traveler craves mutton and eats with unseemly hunger; the Space Traveler avoids meat.

Let me conclude by making the bold argument that *Perelandra* has a better constructed plot than either of his two models. There is no plot to speak of in David Lindsay's *A Voyage to Arcturus*: the traveler awakens naked on the immense planet, and after being rescued and treated with saintly hospitality by Adam-and-Eve-like figures of Tormance, named Panawe and Joiwind, he travels with no discernible purpose through eight or ten highly symbolic landscapes, and then dies or is reborn.

The plot in *The Time Machine* is well constructed, since it takes the form of a mystery. The Time Traveler lands in the shadow of the Sphinx of the far future, and slowly, after several red herrings, comes to realize the true horror beneath, literally beneath, the Edenic gardens and palaces of the soft and nigh-sexless Eloi. But there is no dialog with any of the inhabitants of the future world, and no character arc, and no resolution of the plot. The Time Traveler has no more power to save the Eloi than you have to save all the zebra in Africa from the claws of the lioness. The resolution, to put the matter another way, is to answer the riddle of the Sphinx: the news of the Time Traveler is that man is an animal like all others, subject to the remorseless and blind process of Darwinism, and in those teeth of the gears of evolution, neither intelligence nor spirit is especially prone to be maintained.

And there is not the least trace of humor or whimsy, nothing akin to Ransom trying to talk to a dumb beast he thinks may be a Venusian, in either the Time Traveler nor Maskull, and there are very few traces of ordinary human personality.

Upon rereading, I noticed how tightly the plot of *Perelandra* is actually constructed, which as a youth I thought was somewhat meandering and talkative. It is a mystery and adventure in three acts, and the greatest mystery, not revealed to the end, is to know to what end Ransom is being sent to another world.

Consider that any reader not spoiled by reading essays such as this beforehand do not know what kind of world Perelandra might be when Ransom first wakes upon its waves. The intense physical pleasures of every act are remarkable, as is the beauty of the ever-changing landscape, and the unexpected friendliness of the wildlife. The scene where he tries to speak to one of the Hesperidian dragons is played for laughs, but it is actually quite arresting and tense; as is the scene where he spots a human figure in the distance and fears he is hallucinating, and so runs up and down the valleys of the floating island, and as if in a dream, the valleys become hills with every passing wave. But the mystery of what sort of world this is, and why he is there, is heightened.

We then discover the psychology of the Green Lady is more strange than that of Sorn or Hross on Mars: the idea of introspection is so new to her that she is dumbstruck. It is not without an eerie sense of recognition that the reader realizes this is what the mind would be like which no one, save perhaps the Twelve Disciples, ever met on Earth: a mind utterly innocent, utterly without guilt. And yet, like the Adam and Eve of Milton's *Paradise Lost* (on which the drama is also molded) she is highly intelligent, and so virtuous and pure as to be unaware of her own virtue and purity. Lewis displays this in convincing details, including such small matters as how she sits or stands, or how she does not know how to converse with two people at once.

The next revelation is that she is the Eve and Mother of her world, a queen, and the moment when she seeks to send greetings to her sister, the Queen of Earth, Eve, mother of the Human Race, by way of Ransom—only to have him awkwardly and with much shame explain that his mother is dead—few enough are the scenes in any science fiction story which capture this flavor of strangeness and wonder and recognition. For the character of the Green Lady leaps as if alive from the page and the reader says, "Of course that is what such a creature would be like, if only she were real!" Of course.

The descent and appearance of Weston is the next surprise, as is the horrific tale of his possession by entities he describes as a Shavian "Life Force" but which Christians and men of all faiths will recognize as a chthonic and unclean spirit. Only a modern materialist is so naïve as not to recognize the devil when he introduces himself and asks to share and consume your soul.

The scenes of the Un-Man tempting the Lady and tormenting Ransom are, upon rereading, rather brief and to the point, and Ransom's despair of out-arguing the devil seems quite a bit more realistic when I read it as an adult. Ransom is physically exhausted and the devil is too subtle for him. As a youth, I was too optimistic to believe that the spoken truth could not convince. As an adult I know better. And so comes the dread and final decision to trample the serpent of this unearthly Eden, and crush his head even as he bites Ransom's heel.

In a most satisfying climax, Ransom climbs out of the underworld, finds his way to a high and holy mountain, and there is the presence of beasts and angels and the Lord and Lady of the newly-saved world, Ransom hears not only the explanation for why these terrible deeds were necessary, but why life and the cosmos are necessary, far more than he could have thought to ask.

The major dislike of those readers who dislike the work is centered on two final scenes: first, where Ransom is commanded by the silent pressure of the Divine Will to murder Weston in cold blood. It seems unconstitutional to suppress the devil's freedom of speech, if not downright unchristian to murder him. With this viewpoint I have so little sympathy, I am not sure I can rebut it with justice. I would feel the same way about some environmentalist who objected to Van Helsing putting a stake through the heart of Dracula on the grounds that vampires are an endangered species. The idea that Christians should all be monks and pacifists no doubt would delight the Axis Powers with whom the civilized nations of the world, along with Soviet Russia, were locked in mortal struggle, the bloodiest war in history, and one in which more hung in the balance than merely a question of sovereignty or prestige. I am reminded that this war was ongoing when the book was written.

I will also remind the reader that Weston, in a particularly horrific scene near the very end, is allowed by the devils occupying him to rise to the surface, peer out through human eyes again, and address Ransom in a human voice. Ransom very wisely suggests Weston pray—a child's prayer if he cannot recollect a man's prayer—but Weston never makes the least attempt to save himself from being consumed and obliterated. Ransom speculates that, unlike the divine light which grants even more individuality to each soul as that soul is loved, the darkness of hell makes the boundary between devil and possessed soul blurred, indistinct, meaningless. In effect, Ransom kills the body of a man already dead.

The second scene is the vision of the Great Dance, which is one of the most well-crafted, briefest, and most powerful prose poems of the Christian view of life and the universe ever penned. That it is set in the midst of an eerie space adventure story lends a certain unexpected dignity to the work. I can understand how those who hate all things Christian would hate or skip this passage, but as a work of science fiction, it is a description of both the transcendence of what a nonhuman but superhuman intelligence might think, and a description of a point of view even more alien to modern and fallen man than anything uttered by men from Mars.

If you cannot tolerate alien points of view, dear reader, you have no business reading science fiction. If you want nothing that threatens, nothing that provokes, nothing with which you disagree, or which disagrees with you, just watch television.

10

NIGHTFALL AND NIGHT LAMP

SCIENCE FICTION IS a particularly adroit tool for examining human nature, more adroit than, say, the allegedly realistic modern novel, because it allows the author to introduce the changes society is likely to suffer as various technologies, speculative or fantastic to us now, make their advent on Earth. Only the least thoughtful of science fiction writers can introduce such staples of the genre as the superhuman, the robotic or artificial intelligence, the non-human alien, and not lay bare his own foundational assumptions about what it means to be human.

Such unthoughtful science fiction writers will treat, for example, robots merely as comedy relief characters, with all the same foibles and follies as a Bob Hope. The comedy-bot might be shown quaking at the threat of having an apelike alien rip his arms off if he fails to throw a game of holographic chess, but a thoughtful science fiction fan might wonder why a machine would fear the loss of a limb any more than an automobile would fear a tire change. The more thoughtful science fiction fan might wonder why the robot was programmed by his software designer to be craven. An even more thoughtful science fiction fan might conclude that the robot manufacturers and owners receive a cheap yet hollow pleasure from bullying servants designed to cringe. (The most thoughtful science fiction fan of all will notice that the robot being threatened is shaped like a Hoover vacuum cleaner, and has no arms to rip off in the first place.)

Because science fiction allows the extraterrestrial or artificial human or superhuman onstage, it more easily asks and answers the question what it means to be a man, because a contrast between human and nonhuman forces the question to the fore. The science fiction writer almost has no choice but to betray his view of human nature. The thoughtful science fiction writer makes it even more clear.

In this essay, let me discuss two of the more thoughtful, Isaac Asimov and Jack Vance. The contrast is informative, since Asimov can aptly be taken to represent the views of John W. Campbell Jr., whose *Analog* was one of the most influential magazines in the genre; Jack Vance along with Cordwainer Smith appeared in the pages of *Galaxy* magazine under the editorial hand of Frederick Pohl, and owes more to the fantasies of Clarke Ashton Smith or Lord Dunsany than to the technophilia of Gernsbeck or can-do optimism of Campbell.

If Isaac Asimov champions the world view common to 'Hard SF', Jack Vance can serve if unwillingly as the champion of the world view of 'Soft SF', and, contrary to the terminology, I propose to show that Soft SF is more realistic than Hard, at least as far as human characters are concerned.

I have never been convinced of the view of human nature which comes across as the central conceit of Isaac Asimov's novels and stories. Asimov's *Caves Of Steel* proposes that living in overpopulated warrens would make men agoraphobic; in *The Naked Sun*, he proposes likewise that living in robot-run hermitages would make men phobic of being in the same room with another human being. The most famous of these stories of malleable mankind, and his most often reprinted short story, is 'Nightfall' were men raised in a world whose many suns shed eternal sunshine go mad at the first dusk in a thousand years.

On the other hand, I have heard reviewers and critics and commentators say, either with a chortle of delight or with a moue of scorn, that the societies depicted in Jack Vance tales, such as *Night Lamp* or *Emphyrio* or *City of the Chasch*, are overcomplicated, delicate, ridiculous, as fantastical as a Faberge Egg—and I have heard it so frequently, that I cannot bring a single contrary comment to mind. The most famous of these is 'The Last Castle' which concerns a society of aristocrats so haughty and settled in their ways that they cannot bring themselves, even at the expense of their own survival, to do the necessary, sober, and dirty work of defending themselves from a revolt among their slave-creatures.

It has always struck me that Jack Vance's fantastic societies, and the odd ways of the odd men of the odd worlds he has shown us, are not any more fabulous or unusual than real tribes and nations and civilizations which have lived here on Earth, and that his view of man is, at the root, realistic to the point of cynicism. Only the vocabulary he uses to express it is fantastical, and this is the root of his humor, acrid and dry as it is. Jack Vance has mastered the technique of having his characters utter the most selfish and vicious of sentiments in tones of lofty erudition.

It has always struck me that Isaac Asimov is portraying a view of man so mechanically puppet-like and so unrealistic as to be little more than an intellectual exercise. His human beings operate according to simple and unbreakable laws, as obvious and mechanical as his famous Three Laws of Robotics.

Asimov reports the origins of his 'Nightfall' as follows: According to Asimov, John W Campbell Jr prompted Asimov to write the story after discussing a Ralph Waldo Emerson quote:

If the stars should appear one night in a thousand years, how would men believe and adore, and preserve for many generations the remembrance of the city of God which had been shown!

Campbell's contrariwise opinion was: "I think men would go mad."

And the rest is history. Asimov did as credible job with the idea, and added or invented as much scientific sounding nonsense as he needed to make Campbell's ridiculous conceit seem sound. The short story is well constructed, even masterful, as the various scientists begin to uncover an appalling truth about their civilization on a world in a multiple star system that has never known night. By the time the gripping final paragraphs arrive, the spell is complete, and many a reader, even years later, is convinced that people actually would go mad at their first sight of stars.

Of course the conceit is ridiculous and is meant to be. Campbell was being a contrarian, and he meant to be.

Campbell is not just twisting the nose of Emerson or biting his thumb at the divine hand who designed the stars. The whole point of good SF is to create that sensation which Copernicus must have felt when he realized that the Ptolemaic model was wrong, and that the stable earth was spinning and careening around a heliocentric solar system, or the sensation many readers still feel reading Einstein for the first time: a paradigm shift.

Campbell's paradigm shift was the opinion of Freud and B.F. Skinner and other gentlemen sometimes called scientists, whose speculations in recent years have finally begin to come into well-deserved derision, namely, that man is merely a bag of chemicals whose contents are programmed by heredity and environment.

By this modern if not postmodern theory, there is no reason why the stars look sublime to us. It is an accident of genetics, or a blind by-product of cultural or natural forces, or arbitrary. The theory is, if you change the environment, such as to place man on a world with no nightfall, the stars if seen once each thousand years would be as horrific to them as the rising the cryptical and primordial R'Lyeh once each thousand years is to us.

But, of course, men in real life don't act this way. When Leeuwenhoek first looked in a microscope and discovered that tiny animalcules, too small to see, swarmed and multiplied in every drop of water, every grain of sand, he did not go gloriously mad, and rage through the rainstorm screaming to his neighbors that the living creatures were everywhere, in everything. When Cardinal Bellarmine in a famous (and utterly fictional) event, refused to look through the telescope of Galileo, it was not because Galileo, seeing the four satellites of Jupiter, realized that the skies were not the comfortable perfect spheres of Ptolemy, but instead were vastnesses filled with thronging bodies, asteroids and alien earths. Galileo went shrieking and gibbering from house to house, warning that the skies were horrific voids, and Cardinal Bellarmine, wisely avoiding the sanity-shattering truth, recoiled in terror from the telescope. That is exactly what never happened.

In both cases, men were fascinated by the intricacy, glory and beauty of creation, revealed to their awe-inspired eyes by science. The men of Venus would feel the same way when the clouds parted, or the men of Asimov's fictional world whose nightfall was only once in a thousand years. Despite what you may have heard about the Renaissance Church, the

Vatican continued to support the astronomical sciences before and during and after Galileo, and does so to this day.

Now, one might object that the natives of Asimov's fictional world of Lagash were not human beings but aliens, and therefore they well might have the quirk of psychology aforementioned. Maybe so, but if so, the tale lacks all emotional impact, and means as little to us as a tale of some beach-dwelling aliens on a world with a dozen large moons, who once in a thousand years see the tides go out, and, upon viewing the shipwrecks and sunken cities and beached whales and coral stands of the sea-bottom, due to their psychopathological fear of sea-mud, all go suddenly mad.

We earthmen think the stars are sublime, almost too beautiful to be described. That is a fact of human nature. 'Nightfall' only has that Copernican sense of disorienting paradigm shift if we agree with the unspoken premise that we earthmen think the stars are sublime because and only because of our environment.

Asimov wrote a short story along similar lines to 'Nightfall' called 'Strikebreaker', in which a visitor from Earth to an asteroid colony Elsevere discovers that the family in charge of the waste recycling has gone on strike, which threatens the ecology and the life support of the colony. The visitor understands that the recycling officer and his family are shunned, not permitted physical contact with any other colonist due to the irrational custom of the colonists. The officer is on strike to overturn this cruel law. Nonetheless, the visitor descends into the forbidden recycling area, operates the controls, recycles the sewage, and saves the colony. In a grotesque display of ingratitude, the colonials inform him by message that he must exile himself forthwith without seeing or touching anyone else, since he is now untouchable and ritually unclean.

Asimov himself, in an introduction to this tale that he

penned for an anthology, wonders why this story dropped without a ripple into the public readership when 'Nightfall' had made such a splash. My own theory is that 'Strikebreaker' lacks the central element of the vertigo of Copernicus which is the emotional core of 'Nightfall': the message that the beauty of the stars is merely an arbitrary preference, like driving on the right rather than the left side of the highway, and would be horror rather than sublimity when seen through other eyes. By way of contrast, 'Strikebreaker' has nothing like that. The prejudice against the sewer worker is nothing extraordinary, since it is modeled on the rules against the Dalits or Untouchables of India, and, more to the point, and more offensively to American tastes, the prejudice wins and the visitor from Earth is merely a chump.

But please note that, as in other Asimov stories, the prejudice in 'Strikebreaker' is treated in a mechanical fashion, as if it were one of the Three Laws of Robotics. The visitor from Earth is not a member of the shunned caste of waste workers, and has formed no human relationships, no friendship, and no romance, and no guest-host relationship—any one of which would create a natural conflict with the carrying out of the rule, nor is he extended any professional courtesy due to his status, nor is there any concern for any reaction, retaliation, or souring of the relations between Earth and the colony. It is simply a given, as bland and simple as a clue in a logic puzzle: anyone who operates the sewer controls is shunned. End of story.

The story is clever but shallow, like most stories of its type. The characters are simply machines, and any prejudices implanted by their environment are part of their programming. No one from the colony questions the wisdom of the bias against untouchables any more than any Asimovian robot ever questions the wisdom of their prime directive against harming human beings. Robots simply go insane when presented with simple moral choices, such as whether it is allowable to amputate a man's arm to save his life, or shoot a sniper before he shoots, or even arrest a drunk.

Naked Sun and *Caves of Steel* and other tales of Asimov have a similar mechanical view of human nature. Standards and norms and the definition of sanity (so runs this view) are all the product of environment. Change the environment, and human nature changes.

Ironically, the Asimovian attitude of mankind portrays man as particularly unsuited for scientific endeavors. If sanity is a by-product of environment, to land Man on the Moon or float him in freefall is paramount to blasting his sanity. All colonists of alien worlds would be mad things to us. This is hardly an argument for space exploration.

Let us contrast this with Jack Vance, whose societies, at first blush, seem much more baroque and rococo, too intricate and absurd to exist.

Here is Mr. Vance's account of the origin of his Nebula Award winning 'The Last Castle', taken from the preface to that tale in *Best of Jack Vance*:

The germ of this story was contained in an article dealing with Japanese social interactions. As is well known, Japanese society is highly formalized—much more thoroughly so in the past than during the relatively egalitarian times since the last war.

During the nineteenth century, when a samurai deigned to converse with a person of lower rank, each used markedly different vocabularies, with honorifics precisely calculated to the difference in status. When the person of lower degree discussed the samurai's activities or intentions, he used a special convention. Never would he pose a simple question such as: "Will your lordship go boar-hunting tomorrow?" This would impute to his lordship a coarse and undignified fervor, a sweating, earnest, lip-licking zeal, which his lordship would have found offensively below his dignity. Instead the underling might ask: "Will your lordship tomorrow amuse himself by trifling at the hunting of a boar?"

In short, the aristocrat was conceded sensibilities of such exquisite nicety, competences of such awful grandeur, that he need only toy with all ordinary activities, in a mood of whimsy or caprice, in order to achieve dazzling successes.

So, "The Last Castle" concerns a society of somewhat similar folk, and examines their behavior when the society is subjected to great stress.

We will see the same stratified and over-refined society again in such works as 'The Moon Moth' and *Night Lamp.*

What is interesting, if not alarming, about reading of such societies, civilizations where form counts for more than content, where practical matters of life and death are subordinated to ritualized or stereotyped responses or ceremony, is that such portrayals are not unrealistic. One need only crack open a history book to read of periods of decay and collapse, or unfold a newspaper to see the warning signs of similar corruption in the current world.

Now, not every Jack Vance story takes place in the midst of polities ossified to the point of collapse. The tale *Night Lamp,* one of his later novels, does indeed end on a world of antiquated aristocrats living in somnolent splendor on a world outside the galaxy, so that the blazing spiral of the Milky Way shines down on their untended arbors and empty mansions in an otherwise starless sky; but it begins on a world of solidly middle-class sentiment, but whose obsession with microscopically nuanced distinctions of elevation between rival social clubs leads to brutality.

The point here is that the natural human tendency for hierarchy and subordination will not be abolished by the presence of technical competence. It is a common feature of stories in the tradition of Campbell to assume that scientific progress equates to social enlightenment or egalitarianism. Vancean stories make no such unrealistic assumption.

You see, dear reader, the Vancean assumption is the opposite of the Asimovian. The assumption is this: Despite the changes of technology and environment and culture, human nature will not change.

Allow me by way of illustration to pull a single paragraph, curiously memorable, out the voluminous work of Jack Vance to make my point.

The book *City of the Chasch* concerns one Adam Reith, stranded on the far world Tschai orbiting Carina 4269 after his space vessel is shot down by missiles issuing from an unknown source. Here he finds a world inhabited by four technologically sophisticated but inhuman species, each in continual hostility with the other three, and each of which has bred and mutated human beings as servant races, and humans have adopted, insofar as they can, the outlook and psychology of the aliens. The plains and steppes and islands of Tschai are occupied with various independent cities and tribes of men who exist somewhere between the Bronze Age to Victorian Age levels of technology, but no advance beyond early railways or simple radio is permitted by the space-travelling aliens. Hence we have a planetary romance of the Edgar Rice Burrough style, but with a more reasonable conceit than most for having high tech energy weapons alongside rapiers and cutlasses, or having galleons and cogs and caravels plying the winedark sea beneath the silent anti-gravity platforms of air-rafts and stratospheric craft.

The peculiar genius of Jack Vance is showing servant-races of man, cruelly adapted to the purposes of their nonhuman masters, and reacting with the typical human psychological trick of making their own subservience a matter of ceremony, cult, and cant. The Chaschmen, for example, despite the physiological improbability of the event, regard themselves as the larval stage of the Chasch, and wear false craniums to better to resemble their thickset and pangolin-scaled alien masters. The Chasch, to better aid the humans in the convenient self-deception, plant their eggs in the corpses of newly dead human slaves, and claim to be the reincarnations or evolutions of each specific dead man. (The Dirdirmen have a different myth to explain their subservience to the Dirdir, claiming the two species to have evolved from the two halves of a primal egg on the Dirdir homeworld of Sibol; the Wankhmen may have a more clear-eyed view of their own circumstance.)

In this scene, Adam Reith has disguised himself as a Chaschman, and enters their city to reconnoiter. When he is discovered, he desperately eludes pursuit, and while seeking escape through the humbler quarters of the weird alien metropolis, chances upon the following:

His attention was attracted by a tavern in the basement of a tall building. From the low windows came flickering red and yellow light, hoarse conversation, an occasional gust of bellowing laughter. Three Chaschmen came lurching forth; Reith turned his back and looked through the window down into a murky taproom, lit by firelight and the ubiquitous yellow lamps. A dozen Chaschmen, faces pinched and twisted under the grotesque false crania, sat hunched over stone pots of liquor, exchanging lewd banter with a small group of Chaschwomen. These wore gowns of black and green; bits of tinsel and ribbon bedizened their false scalps; their pug-noses were painted bright red. A dismal scene, thought Reith; still, it pointed up the essential humanity of the Chaschmen. Here were the universal ingredients of celebration: invigorating drink, gay women, camaraderie.

There is simply nothing parallel to this in anything in Isaac Asimov that I have read, and I have all of his published science fiction works. Asimov shows no twinge of awareness that the claustrophobic human beings of *Caves of Steel* nor the hermetically isolated hermits of *The Naked Sun* would quaff gin and rum toddy in their hours of relaxation, or seek the company of fair coquettes, or play the lute, or dream great dreams, even if those dreams are shaped by the psychoses of their insane societies.

Again, contrast is key. Isaac Asimov more than other Hard SF authors regarded mankind as a machine open to a technical fix. It is telling that the peoples of his worlds of Lagash and Elsevere talk and act like 1950 middle-class Americans, except for the one change in their psychology caused by the one crucial counterfactual which forms the hook of the story. There the contrast is used for the opposite purpose and drives toward the opposite result as in a Vance yarn: against the bland off-white hue of a culture no different from those of the readers of the time, the one jarring stroke of the social insanity or social inanity gleams like a comet.

Jack Vance paints vivid landscapes of ornate and odd civilizations, with customs as strange to us as those of Tibet, and whether he means to or not, shows the essential similarity of human nature across cultural divides. To be sure, Vance is a master of the fine and ancient art of exaggeration, and the dry drollery of such exaggeration is part of the appeal. The Brahmins of Boston live in rigid conformity to artificial customs, as those of India, but none so rigid and so artificial as those of the worlds of *Night Lamp* and 'The Last Castle'.

But the art of fiction is the art of exaggeration. If you want to read carefully balanced accounts giving each side due proportion, then read a newspaper (preferably an old-time newspaper from the days before newspapers became addicted to exaggeration and hence became fictional themselves). Exaggeration is unrealistic, but it is not unreal.

It is to be noted that Jack Vancean heroes are often

understated, even to the point of being laconic. Against the multicolored landscape and roaring spectacle of strange or eerie absurdity, the wry but competent Vancean hero does his work without drawing attention to himself. Rarely does the protagonist voice or advance a philosophy or worldview alien to that of his readers, or, if he does, he will preach pragmatism, this-worldiness, a desire to avoid excess.

For my taste, the ordinary man in an extraordinary circumstance is the very definition of adventure and romance.

The concept that ordinary men, and the ordinary virtues a common man is called upon to exhibit in extraordinary times, are as they are merely because they were so programmed by the arbitrary or unintentional mechanics of their environment is the very definition of the unadventurous and unromantic.

Aside from the initial sugar-rush of that vertigo of Copernicus, the tale that tells men that they are machines, all their adventures and romances mere illusion and folly, all their deepest beliefs absurd, is a tale that holds no drama, offers no insight, attracts no fascination, rewards no rereading, drains joy, strangles laughter, and gathers darkness.

One can imagine a young man first tasting deeply of the wine of poetry reading the words of Emerson which opened this essay, and walking out of doors at night in some place far from the lights and noise of the city, gazing at the dark high dome of the stars with fresh awe and an awakened sense of spirit, and the greatness of the architect who placed them there, suns mightier than our own, immensely far away, numberless, bright, almost appalling in their transcendent beauty. Such a man could stare at the sky for a lifetime, and still not see all there was.

One can likewise imagine a young man first reading this tale by Isaac Asimov, looking up at the stars he once thought divinely beautiful, and seeing neither hope nor meaning in them, merely something which, if some twist of matter in his brain had been connected by blind change to other molecules, would drive him mad. There would nothing further for him to see.

11

SPACE OPERA, SPIRAL ENERGY, AND THE DARK SIDE OF DARWINISM

THIS ARTICLE WILL START as an anime review for *Gurren Lagann* (known in Japan as Tengen Toppa Gurren Lagann, "Heaven-piercing" Gurren Lagann) morph into a review of *How to Train Your Dragon,* and end somewhere very far from the fields we know, perhaps as a philosophical musing, perhaps as a sermon.

It is filled with spoilers, and pretty annoying spoilers at that, so do not read further unless you want to find out that "Rosebud" is the name of Luke Skywalker's true father. Read at your own risk.

At the welcome recommendation of several people, I sought out *Gurren Lagann.* Those people, to whom I am grateful, correctly judged that it was the same kind of over-the-top Space Opera that I both read and try to write.

Let us pause to deal with the ever-burning question of what differentiates Space Opera from Military SF or any of the related genres. My answer is simple: when you are done reading E.E. 'Doc' Smith's *Skylark of Space* or *Galactic Patrol* and their sequels, or done watching *Star Wars,* and you are still in the mood for a yarn of the same kind, the type of story you seek is what we now call a Space Opera. When you are done reading *Starship Troopers* by Heinlein or *Forever War* by Haldeman, and you are in the mood for the same kind of tale, you seek Military SF.

The defining characteristic of Space Opera is gigantism, larger-than-life characters storming across larger-than-life stages blowing up worlds. Any story where the term "The Battle-Dyson-Sphere opened an aiming aperture wider than the rings of Saturn and ignited all suns in its internal triple star system to Nova-level output" could be inserted without confounding the story, or where the term "Space Pirate" can be used with a straight face, is likely to be a Space Opera. Space Opera usually does not deal with an infantryman's-eye-view of the war: you are reading about the doings of the Gray Lensman, not with the barroom brawls, letters from home, and stoic loneliness of Juan Rico or William Mandella. The short answer is that Space Opera deals with the Achilles and Ulysses of the future, heroes invulnerable or able to outwit the gods themselves, whereas Military SF deals with G.I.'s.

One trick that E.E. 'Doc' Smith perfected was the geometrical increase of scope. In *Skylark of Space*, the duel was between Superscientist Richard Seaton and Evil Superscientist Marc Q. "Blackie" DuQuesne, and both were igniting atomic explosions on planetary surfaces with abandon: but by the fourth book *Skylark DuQesne*, the climax included a scene where countless millions of stars were teleported from one galaxy into the exact location of home suns of evil star systems in a second galaxy, triggering so many supernovae that the entire second galaxy was one smear of spiral super-nova-level radiation while the first galaxy was dimmed, and meanwhile all the good planets of that galaxy were teleported to freedom in carefully selected orbits at the correct distance, each one around the star in yet a third galaxy. Space

Opera often involves this type of one-upsmanship: the whole planet is at stake, the whole solar system, the whole galaxy, the whole cluster, and so on.

Gurren Lagann has this Skylarkian formula perfected. It starts out gigantic and grows larger from there.

Spoilers Ahead! A Plethora Of Spoiling Spoilers!

SYNOPSIS: The story starts with Simon the Digger, who lives in what might as well be the City of Ember, an underground village of tunnels and caves, troubled by frequent earthquakes. He slowly and patiently drills new tunnels needed for the villagers to eke out a pathetic and marginal existence. His outrageously reckless and boastful comrade Kamina tells of a world above the only world they know, a place called "The Surface" where there is no roof and no walls. Then Simon unearths a small but powerful battle-robot, a mecha called Gurran, from the ancient days, shaped like a human face, or perhaps like the scowling facemask of a samurai. It is smaller than a VW Bug.

The activation of the Gurran robot triggers an attack from the surface. A robot shaped like a giant shark face, pursued by a micro-bikini-clad riflewoman with rifle and with womanly parts both absurdly oversized, plunges through the ceiling and into the village.

Battle ensues. When the trio of friends overcomes the sharkbot, they break through the ceiling into the open sky. In a scene of haunting beauty, they see the sun in the west and moon in the east, mingled with the stars and crimson clouds of dusk, as they hang, slowly turning, in midair in their flying bot, winds in their faces, eyes wide with awe.

The miniature battle robot runs on what is called "Spiral Energy" which is ability to turn the stark, burning, hot-eyed and loud-raging passion, willpower, soul, and fighting spirit of the pilot into whatever form of weapon might be needed (usually absurdly gigantic drills). Spiral Energy violates the laws of conservation of matter (by producing weapons out of nothing) and it reverses entropy (by repairing damaged robots). It helps if you scream out the name of the attack before breaking a law of nature.

More battle ensues when the beast-men who dwell on the deserted wasteland of the surface world discover and attack them. The comrades capture a mecha of the enemy, this one taller than a house, and turn it against the beast-men. More battle ensues. They combine their battlerobots into superbattlerobots to fight the evil beast champion Viral, and more battles ensue. The four great generals of Lord Genome each launches assaults against the growing party of adventurers, who have by now become an army of resistance. An even larger mecha, this one the size of an aircraft carrier, attacks and is captured by Simon. They gain and lose allies and friends as the fortunes of war turn. Simon grieves over the loss of his friend Kamina, but saves the young and beautiful princess Nia in a coffin in a dumpheap filled with coffins: she is one of countless clones made by the creator and master of the Beastmen, Lord Genome, she does not at first realize her allegedly loving father was merely a toymaker who wearied of her.

Joined by all the forces now emerging from all the buried villages, whose despair was turned into hope by the example of outrageous courage of the resistance, Simon and the Armies of Man discover the superscraper superfortress of the Lord Genome, a structure shaped like a funnel. This turns out to be yet another mecha, a colossus miles tall. Final battle ensues. As he dies, Lord Genome reveals that he was keeping mankind buried, impoverished, weak and hidden to keep them safe: he hints at an apocalyptic danger should the human population ever reach one million.

Seven years later, in the midst of an era of progress and prosperity, the one millionth baby is born, and secret bases on the moon, programmed by the same coalition of alien races who once defeated mankind, begin to launch attacks. Simon the Digger, now world leader, is blamed for the attacks, betrayed, deposed, scapegoated, imprisoned. First one, then dozens, then countless enemy units descend from space to bombard the Earth; when the aliens degrade the orbit of the moon so that it will spiral into the Earth, even those in the buried cities have no hope to survive.

But that same unyielding and unconquerable spirit, reckless bravery akin to madness, visits Simon even while he is chained in the stinking depth of the prison, peering out through the bars of his jail cell and sees the titanic moon, occupying nine tenths of the sky, beginning to glow with reentry heat. He escapes and gathers the loyal mecha-pilots to attempt in foolishly impossible battle against the Moon! The Earthmen, hopelessly outnumbered, sail an ancient superspacebattleship as large as a city against the alien machines.

The severed head of the corpse of Lord Genome is wired into a biocomputer and questioned. He reveals that man is one of many of the "Spiral Races" whose life processes are based on the DNA spiral of the double helix, but also based on the endlessly ever-upward spiral of Darwinian evolution. The Spiral Races long ago were defeated and hunted almost to extinction by the Anti-Spiral Races, who set in place certain human extinction mechanisms ready to operate the moment Man, or any Spiral Race, again became a threat.

The Anti-Spirals have one single battle strategy which they use in every fight: they allow the humans to think they are doing well, and then suddenly the fighting machines increase in speed and size and power, or another fleet joins the battle, so that all hope is lost. The Anti-Spirals are not seeking merely military victory: they are seeking to quench the human soul in absolute despair.

Battle ensues. The moon turns out to be a fake, merely a moon-colored crust covering a planet-sized ultrasuperspace-battleship. Nia, who is a clone, is therefore not a participant in Darwinian evolution, and therefore is an Anti-Spiral: her brain is possessed by the Anti-Spirals, and she is kidnapped across timespace. Simon uses the Spiral Energy to break a hole in the fabric of timespace just with the force of his willpower, and, seizing control of the moon-sized ultrasu-perspacebattleship, launches a hopeless sortie across all reality in order to seek her.

Battle ensues when the Anti-Spiral Races launch their asteroid, moon, planet, and gas-giant-sized hyperultrasu-perspacebattleships (all shaped like nightmarish scowling faces akin to Easter Island Totems) against the Earthling ultrasuperspacebattleship. Battle both material and psychic ensues, and the crew is drawn into a false reality in the eleventh dimension created from their own minds: it is the law of nature of this artificial reality that no one can escape!

By sheer effort of willpower, certain dead members of the crew spring back to life, and certain pets evolve into intelligent yet furry creatures on the instant, laws of reality are broken, the false universes shatter, and the ultrasuperspace-battleship defeats the hyperultrasuperspacebattleships and finds the hidden fortress-continuum of the Anti-Spiral Race where Nia is held hostage.

The hyperultrasuperspacebattleships of the Spiral and Anti-Spiral races evolve themselves by an effort of willpower into megahyperultrasuperspacebattleships, both now larger than galaxies, and they wade through the stars, flinging spiral galaxies at each other like shruiken, trampling and crushing nebulae constellations, as they clash in hyper-titanic battle. Of course both megahyperultrasuperspacebattleships trans-form into their human-armor shapes, since that is the shape that best summons and controls both Spiral and Antispiral Energy.

Let us pause for a theme song. *Do the Impossible, See the Invisible, Touch the Untouchable, Break the Unbreakable! Raw, Raw! Fight the Power!*

An ornament atop the battle helmet of the megahyperultrasuperspacebattleship-mecha of the Anti-Spirals is the homeworld of the Anti-Spirals.

We see only a glimpse of this gray and waterless city-world, with its countless millions of gray and featureless people lying motionless in cells, perhaps in suspended animation, perhaps in meditation, while the gray and unemotional voice of the Anti-Spiral emissary announces that they were a race once like humans who decided not to evolve, and therefore they keep themselves immortal, motionless, passionless and frozen.

The Anti-Spirals reveal that the use of the Spiral Energy, since it violates the laws of conservation of matter and reverses entropy, cannot help but inevitably increase the mass present in the universe, eventually to create a super-galactic black hole that will absorb the entire continuum, and annihilate all life. It is to prevent this disaster that the Anti-Spirals hunted down to destroy every race possessing the spiral power of evolution.

But that same unyielding and unconquerable spirit, reckless bravery akin to madness causes all the Earthmen, led by Simon, to hurl defiance at this fate, and the Earthmen announce that they will both use the Spiral Energy to continue to evolve ever upward, and to save the universe from the singularity when it occurs!

Victory ensues. The Earthmen return home to the cheers of the entire galaxy. Simon and Nia are married, and in fact he is kissing the bride, when she dissolves into a cloud of motes, smiling sadly. Simon announces that he knew all along his bride had to die when the Anti-Spirals were defeated. One little boy in tears runs up to the hero-widower, and says, "But Simon! We can use the Spiral Energy to resurrect her from the dead! Not one need die!" and with an avuncular chuckle, Simon pats him on the head, saying, "No, boy, the older generation must die in order to get out of thy way for you youngsters to grow and take our place! That is the way of the evolutionary spiral!" And so, with a cheerful shrug, he walks off into the sunset of what is perhaps the worst ending of any good story I have ever seen, ever. Ever, ever.

Don't get me wrong: great anime, I'd recommend it to anyone who shares my taste in outrageous space opera, but the ending dropped the ball at the goal line. Loved the flick; Loved it. Hated the end; Hated it.

GRADE: Four stars!

Semi-Unrelated Philosophical Musings:

So, there I sat, dear reader, looking like Humphrey Bogart in the rain in France with my guts kicked out, thinking unprintable thoughts whose initials happen to be WTF trailed by twenty exclamation points.

I was choking on excess exclamation points because I thought two things:

(1) The Anti-Spirals were entirely right. All along, I was tricked into rooting for the bad guys, who are death-worshiping madmen possessed by a power that will one day destroy the universe.

But (no doubt you are saying) surely Simon and his reck-lessly brave-to-the-point-of-madness friends will live up to their boast and stop the predicted supersingularity from eating the universe, will they not?

To which I say, earlier in the show a severed head of a corpse floating in a glass bucket of nutrient goo reincarnated itself just by a tooth-gritting effort of will, recreating an muscular eight-foot-tall body out of wishful thinking, and now, suddenly, in order to tack an unhappy ending on the donkey-tail of the plot, the humans cannot resurrect the girl all the crewmen suffered and died to rescue from the inter-dimensional dungeon of the Anti-Spirals? How come you can do nine impossible things before breakfast, but not ten?

(2) These are the bad guys from my novel. In *The Golden Age*, there was a group opposed to the practice of immortality, because they wanted the older generation to die and get out of the way. How come the guys who are the bad guys in my book are the good guys in this book?

The answer to both question one and two is the same. The author of Gurren Lagann thought that a happy ending that was too happy would not be suited for the story he wanted to tell. This was a war story, at least of a type, and in war people die.

In theory, this ending should have been no more unsatisfactory because it is bittersweet than an equally melancholy ending for Tolkien's Lord of the Rings. Frodo, having rid the world of the one all-usurping evil that menaced his age of history, is neither honored in his home, nor able to find his ease and happiness on the mortal shores: he must pass into the West, never to return. There are some who sacrifice all in order that others enjoy the fruits of peace.

In practice, however, everything in Tolkien's theme was bent toward a melancholy ending. Everything, large and small, from the willingness of Galadriel to resist the lure of the Ring, and diminish and pass away, to the passing away of all the fine and ancient things of the Middle Earth, to the simple humility of Frodo who takes up the intolerable burden of the Quest with these humble words: "But I do not know the way…" The theme stated over and over in Lord of the Rings is solemn and quiet resolve to persevere despite the absence of any hope.

Gurren Lagann, on the other hand, shouts, screams and bellows its theme over and over again: "We reject common sense to make the impossible possible!" and "Don't you the know who the hell I am?!" Humility and resignation to the inevitable sacrifices of war is nowhere in the ingredients of the heady mix of Gurren Lagann. The theme stated over and over in Gurren Lagann is that an unyielding and unconquerable spirit, reckless bravery akin to madness, can drill a hole in the sky and crack open the heavens themselves.

If you are in the Gurrenoverse, you do not need whatever divine providence it was that aided Frodo as he hesitated, lost and overcome by the lure of evil on the brink of the Cracks of Doom, so that the wretched starveling Gollum, overcome by malice yet spared by compassion, might by the machinations of heaven use evil to bring evil to naught, that good might come of it, when all mortal spirit and will had failed.

No, what you need in the Gurren Lagann universe is unconquerable spirit, the ferocity of King Canute threatening the tide with his sword—because in this universe, the tide, when threatened by a sword, will stagger, crumble, retreat, stagger back, look surprised, and explode.

You don't need divine providence in this universe, because there is none to be had, here: a story where brute willpower and driving passion (not to mention a ferocious attachment of loyalty to your friends) is what you need to prevail is not a story where Providence enters the theme or plot.

As I sat and mused thus, I realized that I had seen this same theme in the last three cartoons, and in each and every samurai or martial arts movie I had seen. Try harder, make sacrifices, be loyal. That was the theme from every tale from *Karate Kid* (any number and either version) to *Speed Racer* to *Pokemon* to *One Piece*.

The difference in emphasis between the degree of sacrifice between the Japanese and the American cartoons and movies is not universal, but it is noticeable: by this I mean it is not in each and every cartoon and show that the Japanese characters are more wounded after the fight, and bury more dead comrades, but it happens often enough that American heroes emerge unscathed, and that even those who seem to be dead pop out of the grave like toaster pop-tarts before the credits roll, that the difference in attitude can be discerned. Americans are both more optimistic, and write more shows with an eye to a sequel.

I also notice a difference in attitude between older cartoons and newer, and this attitude parallels a difference between Japanese Anime and American, in the degree of boasting. Ash Catchem from *Pokemon* has no embarrassment when he tells all and sundry that he meets that he means to be a master in the art of cockfighting with pocket monsters, and likewise the zany pirate chief Monkey D. Luffy from *One Piece* shouts that he is destined to be King of the Pirates as part of his battle-cry. The only American heroes I can think of which follow this self-aggrandizing habit are the Incredible Hulk, who correctly shouts "Hulk Is Strongest Of All!" and an athlete of considerable grace and prowess who unfortunately set the model for the generation of athletes following him, many of whom now boast like the Hulk, Cassius Clay AKA Mohamed Ali. Hosts of talk radio shows followed suit, and boast and swagger and everyone winks as if it were charming.

Sometimes when I see a Japanese cartoon character gritting his teeth even harder, and making his eyes flame even brighter, and he dashes even more swiftly against a giant foe who soundly defeated him last chapter, I am always slightly saddened, because I wonder if the kamikaze pilots in World War Two felt exactly this way. Or, to use an example closer to home, I wonder if the Confederacy thought they could defeat the Union in the Civil War merely by trying harder.

I have nothing against the philosophy that says "If I try harder, if my willpower is like an iron bar, if I train beyond endurance, if I flinch at no sacrifices, then I shall prevail!" It is a pagan philosophy, and, like all decent pagan philosophy, it is noble and melancholy, displaying a resolve won from hopelessness. It is not only a philosophy fit for a man, but one fit for mortal man.

It is philosophy fit for one who is fated to die, because someone who is willing to die but who does not leaves a lingering question. It is not a philosophy fit, for example, for the ending of the Disney version of *The Black Cauldron*, where Gurgi's noble self-sacrifice is unmade by a Lamia-Ex-Machina (this is like a Deus-ex-Machina, except when you lower a witch rather than a god from the stage machinery).

For this reason, I actually have more admiration for Japanese films, like *The Seven Samurai* and its plethora of imitators, American and Japanese, where half the cast is buried in the ground at the end, or even *Legend of the Eight Samurai* (the real name is *Satomi Hakkenden, the Dog-Soldiers of Satomi*, and it was based on a famous Japanese novel sort of the same way *Starship Troopers* was based on a novel of the same name but the opposite in every way). This is a film you likely, dear reader, never heard of, but it is one were everyone in the party is wiped out by the end, except the Princess and her love interest: what we D&D players call TPK = Total Party Kill. But you might have heard of *Davy Crockett* (one of Disney's first live action films) which has a similar melancholy but noble ending. Even Buddy Ebsen, comedy relief sidekick, buys the farm at the Alamo. We last see Davy swinging his empty rifle as a club against the advancing bayonets of Santa Anna's troopers.

For contrast, let me compare this with another movie I've

just watched *How to Train Your Dragon*, which struck me as one of the most tightly plotted children's films I've seen in quite a while. The main character is a spindly, undersized Viking lad named Hiccup with no strength and no skills and no way to fight the dragons who invade his village (which he describes as an old village of all new houses—but the wooden houses all have to be rebuilt after every attack). He is apprenticed to the village blacksmith, and spends his days building weapons and devices of what I can only call "Bronzepunk" level of technology.

In a sequence that is almost wordless of any dialog, we see this loser turn into the village celebrity as he spends his mornings getting to know a wounded Night Fury dragon secretly back to health, and noticing its habits and ways, and spending his afternoons in the dragon training arena, using each little trick he'd discovered to overcome enemy dragons. I have not time to praise this movie well enough: one of the better things I've seen recently.

The comparison I want to make, though, is with the approach. Simon the Digger never once figures a way out of a problem or solves a battle through strategy. He either drives away despair, summons his courage, grits his teeth, and tries harder (and the spiral-shaped will-o-meter shows how much reality-bending battle spirit he can summon up in his heart when he screams his battlecry—this meter over-loads nearly every episode) or some character, and not always a minor character, sacrifices his life.

Hiccup the Viking, on the other hand, never once gets anywhere by trying harder or by training. He circumvents the training with tricks, or, if you prefer, with technology. He knows mechanics and smithcrafty and he becomes the world's first Dracologist, or student of the science of drag-ons. He does not emerge without a scratch after fighting the big bad Mother-of-All-Dragons, but he does get the girl.

We are dealing with two different types of stories here. The first is a David and Goliath story, where the little man slays the Giant in battle, and the second is a Jack up the Beanstalk story, where the little man slays the Giant by outwitting it.

Having a David and Goliath story where half the cast ends up in the ground when fighting the giant makes a certain sense, because the approach is to overcome problems by being willing to make larger and ever larger sacrifices. Having Jack the Giant-killer or the Little Tailor end up in the ground at the end does not make as much thematic sense, because the approach is technological: the point of every technology starting with the lever is to get the maximum effect with minimum effort, that is, to minimize the sacrifices.

Now, since I am fan of paganism (real paganism, mind you, not this neopagan crap) I have no complaint about a war story that ends with tragic grandeur, or even a hero who is an awful braggart if, like Achilles of old, he both lives up to his boasts, and if the story makes clear that such boasts engender the enmity of the gods of Olympus, who allow each hero his moment of shining glory before he falls to the earth, his teeth griping the soil, and his armor clangs on his limbs as he falls. The soul of the pagan is ravined to the underlands, there to twitter like a bat, or captured by cruel and clear-voiced Valkyrie, there to await a battle even more glorious and much more hopeless at the Twilight of the Gods.

I am also a fan of the more modern and American version of heroic tales, where the Death Star gets blown to bits real good, and the heroes fly away to get medals, and no one is in the ground and no one has a scratch.

I am also a fan of Tolkien-style tales, where the littlest and humblest of the dwellers in Middle Earth unseats the vast and mighty power of Mordor, and not through strength of arms. I don't even mind C.S. Lewis stories where the schoolboy kills a wolf with a sword, but it takes a magic lion from beyond the world's end to slay the White Witch: or even a C.S. Lewis-style science fiction story, where bureaucracies in England are destroyed by the curse of Babel from space-angels from Deep Heaven, and heroes merely also serve by standing and waiting.

The first type of tale has a grim Pagan tone, the second a cheery Yankee, the third a humble Christian tone.

So what did I so dislike in the ending of Gurren Lagann? It tried to combine all three tones and it made a discord. The number of minor characters who end up staying dead is a respectable more than half the cast; but the Spiral Energy idea is the idea that sheer optimistic can-do attitude, sheer willpower, can prevail even against the limits of time, space, sense, and reality. And yet again, a stoical resignation to death is the point of the final line; and yet also the idea that Darwinian progress requires death and sacrifice as part of its mindless, ever-grinding millwheel of progress. Those three attitudes don't fit together.

I disliked using Darwinian evolution as the excuse for keeping the heroine dead. Suddenly the boast that the human race was going to figure out a way both to use the Spiral Energy and to avoid the supersingularity to which overuse of Spiral Energy inevitably leads rang false and hollow.

Darwinian evolution, in real life, is a scientific theory, and, as such, has no moral or normative implications. In stories and in art, however, Darwinian evolution is pagan: it is a tale of Wagnerian grimness and greatness where the deaths of all your ancestors, like blood spilled on Aztec altars to remorseless demon-gods, renders you fit for your brief life on Earth: they paid for your evolutionary niche with their suffering and sacrifice. Darwinian evolution, like the blind god Azathoth, by merest chaos brings forth the universe to its present form, but the infinite darkness that came before the unintentional creation of life on Earth did not anticipate us, and the infinite darkness that follows the last death of the last crab, cockroach, or microbe will not mourn nor remember Man any more than it will the cockroach. In stories, Darwinian evolution demands sacrifices as remorseless as the sacrifice of Iphigenia at Aulus beneath her father's knife: the weak and sick and inferior races must die, in order that the master race prevail.

In real pagan stories, the boast of the hero was one of the signs that he was fey and fated to die. In order to make good his boast, the pagan hero needs must don his shining helm of horsehair plume, and stride forth to face Agamemnon, and Ajax, and man-slaying Achilles. The boaster is allowed to boast because he is doomed.

Darwinian evolution in art portrays the theme that a man is doomed because he is meant to be, and one man is meant to die so that the human race will progress to the superman-race or the master-race. Man is mortal so that mankind will be immortal. The individual man is allowed to boast because he is doomed.

Now if, dear reader, you, like me, recoil slightly from the Eugenic implications of Darwinian evolution as it is portrayed in art, or if you are struck with the noble futility and hopelessness of the pagan hero who defies the gods, then I will be so bold as to venture a guess that you fall into one of the two main camps of modern thought: either you are an optimist, who sees infinite potential in the human race for improvement, improvements which are but a few years away, and who regards the idea of sacrifices needed to achieve such triumphs as archaic and absurd; or you are Christian (or a non-Christian who has absorbed some of the Christian world-view unwittingly) who sees man as fallen, a race of that will not regain its true nature and true perfection until after the Parousia, but who regards the sacrifice as having been paid in divine blood at Calvary.

I think either an Optimist would be disgusted at the idea of Darwinian evolution in art, because he scoffs at the notion that it is right for the weak to die to make room for stronger children: and this was basically the notion, if I understood the translation correctly, voiced in the final scene of Gurren Lagann; or that a Christian would be disgusted at the idea that Darwinian evolution in art is a figure of ever more boastful pride and ambition, including a pride that would destroy the whole universe just on the wager than Man will discover a way to break the laws of nature.

Now the reader who also read my book *The Golden Age* (hi, Mom!) might object that the Golden Oecumene pictured in that trilogy was just as ambitious and just as optimistic as any boastful pagan. The Golden Oecumene was a pinnacle of transhuman evolution, was it not?

Ah, but my one reader may not recall the somewhat grim ending of that book. The Golden Age was over, and an Age of War, and Iron Age, was soon to follow. And even the Sophotechs, the supercomputers, of that far future did not foresee any means of living forever, past the heat death of the universe: the Silent Oecumene, who lusted for a more infinite life, and sought a means to escape the laws of entropy and reality, were depicted in my humble tale as the epitome of unreason: creatures not only malignantly irrational, but also irrationally malign.

The Golden Age, if an author can venture an opinion on his own work, is not merely pagan, but stoic, because it was really a story about the limitations of utopia. Many Transhumanists complimented the tale, because it so vividly portrayed some of the technologies in which they place their faith and hope for salvation from death and the limits of the human condition: but one Transhumanist—I cannot recall his name—correctly identified that the tale was not truly Transhumanist in its spirit, because it spoke of the inevitability of death, and the need to resign oneself peacefully, without discontent, to eventual and universal oblivion.

Gurren Lagann was optimistic when it came to the Spiral Energy, the sexual power of the DNA that leads man and civilization ever upward and ever onward, and absurdly optimistic when it came to the question of saving the universe from the pollution side effects of Spiral Energy. It defies common sense and breaks the laws of reality—that is the giddy appeal of the tale.

But then it is stoical, pagan, and melancholy when it comes to the bride of the hero, not to mention the others who fell in war. Death is not only inevitable in the Gurren Lagann universe—that is something any Stoic must with grim and tearless eyes admit—suddenly it is needful to get the older generation out of the path of the ever-upward motion. This idea, no doubt meant innocently enough as a bit of sci-fi techno-talk, had too much of the foetor of Eugenics to it, something of the shadow of the swastika, for this viewer, at least, to continue to suspend his disbelief.

You can save the universe, but you cannot save the girl?

ABOUT THE AUTHOR

John C. Wright is a retired attorney, newspaperman and newspaper editor, who was only once on the lam and forced to hide from the police.

He is the author of some twenty two novels, including the critically acclaimed THE GOLDEN AGE, and COUNT TO A TRILLION. His novel SOMEWHITHER won the Dragon Award for Best Science Fiction Novel of 2016. He has also published numerous short stories and anthologies, including AWAKE IN THE NIGHT LAND and CITY BEYOND TIME, as well as nonfiction. He holds the record for the most Hugo Award nominations for a single year.

He presently works as a writer in Virginia, where he lives in fairytalelike happiness with his wife, the authoress L. Jagi Lamplighter, and their four children: Pingping, Orville, Wilbur, and Just Wright.

Wisecraft Publishing specializes in stories of wonder. It is a supporter of the Superversive Literary Movement.

You can join our newsletter, A Light in the Darkness, here:

Http://eepurl.com/cg-40H

CPSIA information can be obtained
at www.ICGtesting.com
Printed in the USA
LVHW112252280520
656872LV00003B/1099